STORIES IN THE LAND

A Place-Based Environmental Education Anthology

Introductory essay
by John Elder

NATURE LITERACY SERIES

NUMBER 2

THE ORION SOCIETY'S NATURE LITERACY SERIES offers fresh educational ideas and strategies for cultivating "nature literacy" —the ability to learn from and respond to direct experience of nature. Nature literacy is not information gathered from a series of isolated, external "facts," but a deep understanding of natural and human communities. As such, it demands a far more integrated and intimate educational approach. Nature literacy means seeing nature as a connected, inclusive whole. Furthermore, it means redefining community as an interwoven web of nature and culture, a relationship marked by mutual dependence and one enriched and sustained by love. The materials presented in this series are directed to teachers, parents, and others concerned with creating an education that nurtures informed and active stewards of the natural world.

Nature Literacy Series Number 2
ISBN 0-913098-51-5

Copyright © 1998 by The Orion Society.
195 Main Street, Great Barrington, MA 01230
Phone: 413/528-4422 Fax: 413/528-0676
E-mail: orion@orionsociety.org Web: www.orionsociety.org

♻ Printed on recycled paper with soy-based inks.

STORIES IN THE LAND
A Place-Based Environmental Education Anthology

Table of Contents

This monograph and the initiatives described herein have received generous support from the Geraldine R. Dodge Foundation of Morristown, New Jersey. The foundation's president, Scott McVay, and program officer, Alexandra Christy, have demonstrated a solid appreciation for and dedication to the field-based, interdisciplinary nature of Stories in the Land. Their visionary support of these nontraditional educational initiatives has meant a lot to all those involved.

Teaching at the Edge
by John Elder

I n her essay on "Landscape, History, and the Pueblo
Imagination," Leslie Marmon Silko describes how her
Pueblo ancestors "instinctively sorted events and details into
a loose narrative structure." Theirs was an outlook, and a survival strategy, based upon "collective memory." "Whatever the
event or the subject," Silko writes, "the ancient people per-
ceived the world and themselves within that world as part of
an ancient continuous story composed of innumerable bundles
of other stories." The Orion Society's initiatives in environmental education, Stories in the Land, have far more in common with such narratives than they do with the pre-tests, post-
tests, and quantifiability of a formal "curriculum." They grow
out of earlier stories, but are transformed by each new narrator. They look for order in human experience and the world,
but depend upon surprises and reversals for their vitality.

The present publication collects stories from various classrooms and collaborations that have been supported by The
Orion Society. These narratives differ widely, as do the geographic and cultural settings of the classes themselves, and are
not intended as prescriptive in any way. Instead, they are
offered in the hope of inspiring other teachers to carry out
kindred but distinctive experiments of their own.

I have been asked to frame the stories that follow and to
reflect upon the educational principles and implications that
bind them all together. The best way to start, though, seems
simply to add my own story to the bundle. Because I have been
privileged to work with several of The Orion Society's initiatives, including its collaborations with Middlebury College,
with the Bread Loaf School of English, and with the Geraldine

R. Dodge Foundation, my perspective is that of a participant
rather than an observer. Perhaps tracing my own path as a
teacher will thus let me sketch a map that can then be filled
out as others' paths are also inscribed on it in the subsequent
essays. It will also establish the immediate, personal context for
my reflections about how the landscape of these Orion Society
initiatives may be related to the surrounding terrain of
American education.

I joined the Middlebury College English Department twenty-
four years ago, and in one year will receive the asterisk beside
my name in the faculty directory that officially marks me as a
graybeard. Over the years, while I have always enjoyed teaching
the excellent students attracted by our English major, I have also
found myself increasingly drawn toward the more interdisciplinary approach of environmental studies. This shift of emphasis
has not unfolded with the premeditation or clarity of a plan, but
has rather been a process of evolution—its direction never
wholly visible at any one stage but describable in retrospect.

While there are growing numbers of people today preparing specifically for careers in environmental education, there
have also been many like myself who've wandered into this
field from backgrounds in diverse areas of the arts and sciences.
For me, such a trajectory has felt like the fulfillment of my
study of literature rather than a turning away from it. Similarly,
environmental education has seemed less a new discipline than
a recovery of the connections from which disciplines originally
emerged, and which they sometimes now impede.

While my teaching specialty was originally British
Modernism, over the first decade of my work at Middlebury it
tilted toward English and American literature that placed a special emphasis on nature. The interweaving of Vermont's natural
beauty with its human history and settlements was one big
influence on the evolution of my educational vision. The
dense, third-growth woods clothing the Green Mountains
today also contain a burgeoning animal population. The deer,
bear, beaver, and bobcat which have long been part of our
mid-Vermont ecology have been joined, in the two and a half
decades since our family moved here, by moose and cata-

mounts making their way down from the northeast part of the state. When I was a boy in northern California I had to drive several hours to reach the Sierra Nevada; in Vermont I can walk out our back door in the village of Bristol and find moose and bear sign not half an hour up the slope. Living in such a landscape has forced me to rethink my sense of wilderness and culture as separate categories. Signs of human habitation such as cellar holes, stone walls, and choker cables abound under the majestic canopy of maples, beech, and pine. Vermont's is both a haunted and a recovering landscape. It has stimulated my appetite for stories in the land, and shaped the direction of my reading and teaching.

Wordsworth and Frost were the first writers who helped me to appreciate this Vermont landscape more vividly and who, simultaneously, led me to rethink my teaching. Neither focuses on wilderness so much as on the human dramas rooted in particular natural scenes and environments. These two great poets locate their ballads of disruption and revelation along the ragged margins of mountain settlements. The richness of their poems resembles what ecologists would call an "edge effect," and this is in fact one of the concepts I've found most helpful as a teacher of literature and the environment.

Where two ecosystems meet, an "ecotone" is produced along their common boundary—a zone containing some species from each constituent environment, as well as species distinctive to that interface. Such an ecotone has both a greater number of species and a greater density of organic life than the surrounding ecosystems. Edges are always moving, and it is their dynamic character that makes them both unusually rich in nutrients and

chancy. This is true educationally as well as in a biological
sense. An individual venturing over the line in the quest for
life more abundant may well end up as a meal for some pioneer venturing in from the other direction. We'll need to be
nimble in order to take advantage of new interdisciplinary
opportunities, and ready to relinquish our newer categories,
too—such as "environmental education"—when they are no
longer as appropriate to the shifting ecotone.

Two contemporary poets who did a lot to help my teaching become edgier were Gary Snyder and A. R. Ammons. I was
inspired by Snyder's sense of continuity between Asian and
Native American spirituality, and by the tempered optimism
fostered by his broad geological timeline. The long, pulsing lines
of Ammons's poetry expressed an ecstatic view of science. His
insights into ecology and physics, particularly, helped me look
beyond the "two cultures" enshrined in the separate science and
humanities divisions of the college curriculum. Snyder and
Ammons have continued to frame my teaching, and have
inspired me to explore the work of other contemporary poets.
Mary Oliver, William Stafford, and Pattiann Rogers are among
those who are especially impressive to me, because of their
grounding in closely rendered landscapes and their capacity for
fierce and loving attention to the processes of this world.

I also found literary ecotones in Thoreau and the
American nature writers inspired by his work. Informed by
science but open to the spiritual and personal meaning of
nature, these essayists integrated their own stories with the
unfolding story of the earth. One contemporary book that had
special meaning for me was Annie Dillard's *Pilgrim at Tinker
Creek*, which I read for the first time in 1979. Dillard's incan-
descent passage on "the tree with the lights in it" made me
long for such a quality of vision in my own experience; it was
both an eloquent piece of writing and a personal revelation
with motivating power. It crossed a line into my life. Realizing
that there was a rich and continuous tradition of such writing
in English influenced my sense of literature and the teacher's
vocation. With Gilbert White in England and Thoreau in
America as important early references, this line of writers
would include, among many others, John Burroughs, John

Muir, Mary Austin, Aldo Leopold, Rachel Carson, Peter
Matthiessen, Edward Abbey, Ann Zwinger, Richard Nelson,
Robert Michael Pyle, Gary Nabhan, Annie Dillard, Gretel
Ehrlich, Scott Russell Sanders, and Terry Tempest Williams.

All of these writers hit me hard, and they changed my
sense of the English curriculum. At Middlebury, as at most
other colleges, we had emphasized the three categories of
poetry, drama, and
fiction, with nonfic-
tion a secondary area
studied mostly as his-
torical background to
"imaginative" writing
or in composition
courses. But I began
to feel that the per-

> **Environmental education seems less a new discipline than a recovery of the connections from which disciplines originally emerged.**

sonal essays produced by American nature writers were as rich
on the levels of language and metaphor as they were charged
with emotion, and as spiritually uplifting as any literature I
knew. This literature was incomparably more inspiring than the
airless, dysfunctional world of so much recent fiction and the
formulaic self-absorption too often prevailing in today's poetry.
Additionally, it was more attentive than the other literature I
knew about from any era to the aesthetic and spiritual implications of science. Contemporary nature writers have bridged
the chasm between the "two cultures."

"Visions of Nature" is the course I introduced at
Middlebury that expressed this emerging interest in environmental literature. It explored the affinities between English
Romanticism, the Thoreauvian tradition, and the work of contemporary poets like Snyder, Ammons, and Oliver. It connected such writing with painters like Constable, Church, and
O'Keeffe and with photographers like Ansel Adams and Eliot
Porter. As the syllabus has varied and developed over the past
decade and a half, it has also frequently included fiction by
William Faulkner, Wendell Berry, Leslie Silko, and other novel-
ists who possess a vivid sense of landscape.

A note of political realism is called for at this point. The
English department was originally unwilling to count "Visions

of Nature" as one of my offerings, since it was judged to be
superfluous to our core curriculum in poetry, drama, and fiction. The first three years of its life therefore required the sponsorship of an NEH grant, with that money paying for a "stan-
dard" English course to replace the one I was not teaching.
Subsequently, though, "Visions of Nature" has been accepted as
part of my teaching load and has also become one of the introductory courses for Middlebury's interdisciplinary environmental studies program. It's my guess that—as with the environmental initiatives sponsored by The Orion Society with funding
from the Geraldine R. Dodge Foundation—there is typically a
need for outside sponsorship or intervention before a new ele-
ment can be introduced into an established curriculum.

Beginning to conceive of literature differently, and to take
different approaches in my own teaching, were the first
changes in my work at Middlebury College. From them have
flowed the recent, more interdisciplinary and collaborative
aspects of my teaching. It's important to emphasize, though,
that while my own path into environmental education has led
through teaching English at a college, this is an ecotone colo-
nized by people who've started in biology, in geography, or in
education. The landscape of connection is not where we started, but where we meet, and I am grateful to the poets and
nature writers who led me to the edge where this exciting
dialogue is taking place.

The environmental studies program at Middlebury offers
the oldest ES major in the country, introduced in 1965. But,
like many such programs, it was for years essentially an applied
ecology track of the biology department, including a few cog-
nate courses in other science and social science fields but no
humanities component at all. When Stephen Trombulak of
biology took over as director of ES a dozen years ago, however, he vigorously recruited me and other nonscientists to help
him develop a genuinely interdisciplinary program. From that
point I found that more and more of my professional associa-
tions, on campus and off, were with people in biology, geology,
political science, religion, economics, and geography, instead of
just with colleagues in English. My office moved out of the
main humanities building, first into a house where students

with a special interest in environmental issues had established a cooperative, and then into a newly designated ES building. Six years ago, when I began a term as director of ES, mine became a split appointment between English and environmental studies, as it remains to this day.

At the same time that the evolution of the ES program at Middlebury was changing the context of my teaching, the community associated with *Orion* Magazine was providing a new source of creative inspiration. The magazine's beauty, idealism, and spiritual emphasis were wonderful antidotes to an academic era in which big claims for meaning were smugly deconstructed. As the Orion community has grown and developed, giving rise to The Orion Society, it has become the focal point for a wide range of events—from the Forgotten Language Tour to the Watershed conference at the Library of Congress—that hold our modern institutions to higher standards of responsibility. Just as my sense of teaching and the college curriculum have been shaped by Middlebury's environmental studies program, my educational values and religious values have been informed by the conversations and the literature generated under Orion's aegis.

If teaching English in Vermont led me to appreciate certain grounded lineages in literature, and if participation in the environmental studies and Orion communities helped me place my literary background in service to interdisciplinary communities of effort, then the Stories in the Land and Watershed Partnerships initiatives of recent years have seemed like first, tentative steps toward models of education that go *beyond* the interdisciplinary.

The writer and ethnobotanist Gary Nabhan, resisting the marginalization that he felt in the term "nature writing," jokingly remarked before one of his readings that it might be better now simply to refer to books on the same shelf with Thoreau, Leopold, Carson, and Williams as "literature" and to books on the other shelves as "urban dysfunctional writing." I'd like to suggest in a similar spirit of playful seriousness that we now conceive of "environmental education" simply as "education"—in contrast to the disciplinary compartmentalization and abstraction that often characterize conventional curricula. My sense of this contrast relates to two things that have been confirmed by Stories in the Land and the Watershed Partnerships: education is most productive at an edge, in the ecological sense; and the beginning of education, as of an environmental conscience, is love.

Rather than assuming that science and the humanities must remain forever discrete, environmental education needs more boldly to inhabit the ecotone where they join and commingle, where something new may evolve. In *The Edge of the Sea*, Rachel Carson uses four telling adjectives to describe the rich convergence along her beloved Maine coast. She says that "the edge of the sea is a strange and beautiful place." She continues: "[Since] for no two successive days is the shore line precisely the same...[it] remains an elusive and indefinable boundary." These four terms may help us to understand the character and promise of environmental education as it evolves in this Orion ecotone.

Successful education has the power to make the world strange again. Without any stake in the places where we live, we walk through days in which there are trees but no tree in particular, we drive along roads that could be anywhere, never registering the mountains to the east and lake to the west that determined, in fact, exactly where that route would run. Such casual familiarity is the opposite of intimacy and attentiveness. When I think back to the defining moments in Stories in the Land and the Watershed Partnerships, they

> **Everything looks different, including the meaning of education, when we bear in mind that the world is beautiful.**

often seem to have been sudden glimpses of a real world, out of alignment with our expectations and therefore restoring three-dimensional solidity to the landscape.

I remember walking in the woods near Bristol with Steve Bless's sixth-grade class from Monkton and an expert tracker named Sue Morse. We were bushwhacking along a narrow slope when one little boy spotted something really strange in a tree. It took everyone a moment to figure out what it was—a big, disheveled porcupine blinking mildly down at us from a crotch in the tree where it had been napping. Every kid's (and adult's) jaw dropped, our eyes widening in surprise at the spectacle of that large animal swaying above our heads—an unexpected life in an unexpected place.

In his *Interpretation of Dreams*, Freud describes dream images as *das Unheimliche*, "the uncanny." They are, he says, both familiar and surprising; their origin may have been a psychological impulse to disguise complicated emotions and motivations, but their promise, if careful attention is paid to them, is to reveal unsuspected connections and liberate creative, happy energies that may have been blocked. The woods, and the edge between science and the arts, are full of arresting dreams.

I once had a colleague at Middlebury College named Bill Glassley who was both an outstanding geologist and a person of strong aesthetic responses. In his desire to convey the beauty of his science he once photographed the mineral sections which, under a microscope and with the aid of polarized light, revealed the defining crystallography of certain minerals. Then he had these incredible close-ups expanded into poster-sized photographs for the lounge where many geology students did their homework. He wanted them to see for themselves the sensuous, intricate designs that embodied the principles and equations of their textbooks. These huge compositions of red and mauve and green were almost comically overt, like the in-your-face portraits of flowers through which Georgia O'Keeffe tried to make the sensuality of her desert world inescapable, and overwhelming. A shift of perspective—up into the trees, down into a crystal or a blossom—makes the world strange enough to get our full attention. It propels us beyond the conventional surfaces and distinctions of what Dewey calls the realm of "inert ideas," making everything new.

Another moment of memorable strangeness came when my Middlebury College seminar that was part of the Watershed Partnerships went to the Bread Loaf campus for an afternoon workshop on field sketching with Clare Walker Leslie. It was a day of laughter and looking closely. But as we completed our final exercise, lying on the grass and drawing the layered outlines of woods, mountains, and clouds, several people noticed simultaneously that the setting sun was high-lighting strands and hammocks of spider webs that swung from the tips of grass blades in such abundance as to transform the dark green lawn of Bread Loaf into a shimmering canopy. When the wind arose, these catenary loops of silver flexed into iridescence. Drawing out of doors had already helped us see a world of buds and clouds, and now let us in for a revelation of the unregistered beauty that always and everywhere surrounds us. Such an experience can raise an educational community to a new level of expectation, and can help every individual in it cultivate more sustained attentiveness. Everything looks differ-ent, including the meaning of education, when we bear in mind that the world is *beautiful*.

The sense of beauty is fostered, thus, by the experience of the world's strangeness, and both are closely allied with what Carson called "the sense of wonder." In her book of the same title, she connects these values in a way that bears not only on primary education, but also on the vitality of education at the secondary, college, and graduate levels:

> If facts are the seeds that later produce knowl-
> edge and wisdom, then the emotions and the
> impressions of the senses are the fertile soil in
> which the seeds must grow. The years of early
> childhood are the time to prepare the soil. Once
> the emotions have been aroused—a sense of the
> beautiful, the excitement of the new and the
> unknown, a feeling of sympathy, pity, admiration
> or love—then we wish for knowledge about the
> object of our emotional response.

We wonder at the world's amazing variety, and we love it for its beauty. These truths are at the heart of attentiveness to nature, and we educators need to assert them with some defi-ance in the face of disciplines that pride themselves on their presumptive objectivity.

I revere the scientific method, with its effort to arrive at unbiased and reproducible results, and its quest for a universal language. But when the language of scientific objectivity is bandied about too glibly it can suggest that we are capable of achieving observations in which there is no observer. The highest, and most trustworthy, science arises when the scientist is also capable of expressing in a personal voice the love that motivated his or her lifetime pursuit of knowledge about volcanoes or snakes or the origin of the universe. It's true of science, as Saint Paul declared it to be of good works, that without love it is as sounding brass or a tinkling cymbal. We need to pay close

Loving attentiveness to one's bioregional community is a discipline, in the sense of being a life's study.

attention when a scientist of E. O. Wilson's stature speculates about the principle of "biophilia," the innate sense of love and admiration for other forms of life that he sees as the basis of biology.

It's not only in the natural sciences that a false objectivity has sometimes hampered feeling education. The study of economics has increasingly dominated our thinking about issues of social justice, national development, and governmental policy. But its premise of universal acquisitiveness is in my opinion a dubious one. As David Orr has remarked, "Economics is the gerrymandered discipline, its boundaries drawn so as to exclude all relevant questions of value." I risk seeming to rant here because it is in comparison with the natural sciences and quantifiably oriented social sciences that fields such as environmental studies and environmental education are sometimes declared to be "soft core"—a haven for tree huggers. I would propose, though, that hugging trees, with all the emotional engagement with nature that it implies, is a worthy activity. Saying this, I fear the gold tassel will be ripped right off my mortarboard. But perhaps, after all, tree hugging is no more deplorable than asserting that greed is the fundamental human motivation or that scientific research should be devoid of human significance or coloration.

Love is where attentiveness to nature starts, and responsibility toward one's home landscape is where it leads. Aldo

Leopold summed it up this way in his essay "The Land Ethic":
"It is inconceivable to me that an ethical relation to land can
exist without love, respect, and admiration for land, and a high
regard for its value." The love, respect, and admiration to which
Leopold refers are the natural outgrowths of a sense of wonder. They are a recognition of deep affiliation with the "land,"

by which Leopold means not
only the soil but also the whole
web of life which it supports.

An approach to education
that begins with love is a
romantic pedagogy. It is opposed
to the classical, or deductive,
model that impresses knowledge, in the different cookie-
cutters of each discipline, on the
amorphous mind and sensibili-
ties of children and the otherwise insufficiently formed. A
romantic or inductive approach
assumes that the capacity to rec-
ognize natural patterns and the power of creative expression
are innate. I don't mean here to value the romantic impulse
exclusively, but rather to suggest that, when facing the environmental challenges of our day, it can be a helpful corrective
to the hermetic tendencies within more classical and deductive disciplines. To the extent to which it becomes established, this model of environmental education will itself
require a counterbalance. But our pressing need now is for a
pedagogy that exposes people to the range of their possible
relationships in the world, and that gives them the language
and models to explore and express such affiliation within a
vivid community of values.

If this sounds strange or unworkable, perhaps the problem
is not with the romantic approach itself but rather with the
impoverished educational context and the mutual distrust to
which we have become accustomed. There is no contradiction
here with the insights of science. On the contrary, it makes the
findings of science more meaningful and more memorable. A

beautiful expression of this compatibility comes in the chapter called "Burrowing Owls" from Terry Tempest Williams's *Refuge*. The narrator's grandmother is a wonderful educator, who takes pains to give the little girl of that chapter a sense of the emotional and symbolic meaning of a bird about which they have been hearing a scientific description: "'When an ibis tucks its head underwing to sleep, it resembles a heart. The ibis knows empathy,' my grandmother said. 'Remember that, alongside the fact that it eats worms.'"

Love is the deepest science, but it is not quantifiable. Loving attentiveness to one's bioregional community is a discipline, in the sense of being a life's study. It does not, however, depend upon the sort of specialized vocabulary that those academic categories we call "disciplines" use to define and defend themselves. There is already a temptation, given the rapid growth of interest in environmental issues, to segregate environmental studies or environmental education into new departments or programs of their own. But we should resist this impulse. The essence of environmental education is a certain energetic waywardness with regard to compartmentalization and boundaries of all kinds.

One revelation of Stories in the Land and the Watershed Partnerships for me has been that often, the most whole-hearted and integrated teaching occurs in the lower elementary grades. Instead of always having schools and colleges looking up the line to the specialized and professionalistic standards of graduate schools, I would recommend that they also try to emulate the best first-grade classes, where music, art, and literature flow directly into the studies of science and mathematics.

The stories that follow in this collection describe several Orion Society-supported experiments in environmental education where this confluence has been been achieved. These endeavors are related but distinct, sharing four fundamental themes:

• ATTENTIVENESS TO STUDENTS' HOME LANDSCAPES. Rather than focusing on problems or controversies, or on exotic landscapes, pursuing a sense of place provides a solid grounding for interdisciplinary study.

• THE CONVERGENCE OF NATURAL SCIENCES AND THE ARTS.
Drawing, writing, identifying plants and animals, and studying
processes of biological succession all help students to see more
vividly the forests that surround their village, or the tidal zone
along their shore, or the currents of life that flow through their
city, through every city.

• TIME SPENT OUT OF DOORS. Both fieldwork of a systematic,
experimental sort and excursions that foster habits of exploration and attentiveness are included in this category.

• HUMAN CONNECTIONS. Exploring cultural aspects of the
community affirms that human history is integral to the natural
history of a landscape. Partnerships between students and teachers at different educational levels, as between the generations in
a given town, have proven to be particularly helpful reminders
that the sense of community is essential to the sense of place.

Another way to characterize these narratives is to say that
the wholeness of a local watershed can repay the attention of
students at every educational level and engage every aspect of
the arts and sciences. A celebrated list of twenty-seven questions was published in *The Co-Evolution Quarterly* and reprinted
in the Sessions and Devall book *Deep Ecology* under the head-
ing "Do You Know Your Bioregion?" It asked readers if they
could do such things as trace their drinking water from precipitation to tap, name five native edible plants in their region, and
tell where their garbage goes. In light of the experiences of
teachers and students in The Orion Society's educational initiatives, I would venture the following list of eight "stories in the
land," inspired by the original twenty-seven questions. These
are the stories that can foster an educational approach more
firmly rooted in our home landscape, wherever that may be:

1) the geological processes producing the main landforms of
our watershed;
2) its characteristic climate, seasons, and weather;
3) the lifecycles and habitats of notable local plants and animals, and the communities to which they belong;

4) the fluctuations of forest history in our region;
5) indigenous human cultures, and some of their own stories about the area;
6) immigration and settlement from other countries;
7) nearby farms and their products;
8) ways people in the watershed presently make their living.

Whether considered by a class of first graders exploring the playground around their school or in a graduate seminar connecting the writing of Robert Frost with the landscape of Vermont, these stories will always be compelling, always new.

The Stories in the Land initiatives have shown that such an integrated and deeply satisfying pedagogy can work. It is nothing as fixed or predictable as a "curriculum," in the sense of a step-by-step program of instruction with quantifiable measures of progress. Rather, this approach to environmental education must be a perpetual process of discovery, celebration, and community. Rachel Carson is not disappointed, after all, that the edge of the sea remains "elusive and indefinable." Rather, that fact represents for her a perpetual escape into the wonder of the world's unfolding presentness. Both Carson and the teachers whose stories follow can celebrate with the poet A. R. Ammons, in his own walk along the shore in "Corsons Inlet," that "tomorrow a new walk is a new walk."

John Elder *is Stewart Professor of English and Environmental Studies at Middlebury College in Vermont. He serves on The Orion Society's board of directors, and as director of its Stories in the Land Initiatives. He is the author of* Imagining the Earth, Following the Brush, *and, most recently,* Reading the Mountains of Home.

Stories in the Land Fellowships

S tories in the Land teaching fellowships are one-year stipends designed to help teachers foster an effective education of place, inspired by The Orion Society's interdisciplinary environmental education models. These programs were developed principally with John Elder, a current member of the Society's board of directors and a long-time advisor and contributor to its publications and programs. Important contributions were also made by Orion Society advisors Scott Russell Sanders, Barry Lopez, David Orr, Gary Paul Nabhan, and others.

The fellowship program was initiated in 1992 when Dr. Elder asked us to consider working with his summer M.A. students at Middlebury College's Bread Loaf School of English, most of whom were secondary-school teachers. The group was studying environmental literature and many wanted to use similar material in their home classrooms the following year, but were hindered by a lack of institutional backing and financial resources for implementing such an unconventional curricular approach.

We responded by inviting these teachers to apply for fellowships, requesting from each a dynamic curriculum plan that made effective use of place-based literature. We asked for a proposal that included: interdisciplinary study of the local natural and cultural history; extensive field experience; frequent use of diverse "human resources" (writers, artists, ecologists, conservation activists, town elders); and a budget for activities and materials specifically suited to their environment.

As we had hoped from the outset, our connections with these teachers were rich and exciting. Occasional phone conversations and site visits combined with regular progress reports from the teachers clearly demonstrated the program's promise. The following year, we decided to again award fellowships but this time invited applicants from the broader Orion community of teachers through an announcement in *Orion* Magazine. The second year's recipients constituted another talented and creative group and again their efforts met with tremendous success. We decided then to make the fellowship program a continuing effort.

Each year since, application guidelines have been made available in late May, with the selection of recipients occurring in late August. In making selections, we seek geographic and cultural diversity, a range of educational and disciplinary backgrounds, and creativity of educational approaches. To date, we have worked with over fifty teachers from every geographic region of the United States as well as several foreign countries. The continued stream of qualified applicants and the dedicated work of fellowship recipients reinforce our sense that these fellowships are an important vehicle for changing the structure and approach of environmental education from the ground up.

During the summer of 1996, The Orion Society convened the first Orion Institute on literature, writing, and place at the Bread Loaf campus, directed by John Elder with visits by several writers and naturalists including Clare Walker Leslie, Robert Michael Pyle, Scott Russell Sanders, and Ann Zwinger. Ten students were selected and enrolled in a pair of interdisciplinary courses based on the literature of place, and each was given a fellowship to adapt these ideas to their home environment.

These fellowships, and particularly those awarded in conjunction with Orion Institutes, are helping to broaden the reach of the Society's educational models. The stories that follow in this volume are prime examples of the ingenuity and perspicacity of the teachers who have used the Stories in the Land teaching philosophy to create vital and probing academic inquiries into their home territory. It is our hope that by presenting this diverse array of stories and sample activities from former teaching fellows, we will encourage others to venture down this innovative and hope-filled path to nature literacy.

Laurie John Lane-Zucker, *Managing Director*
Jennifer Sahn, *Assistant Director*

Science and Stories in a North Philadelphia Neighborhood
by Mark Basnage

George G. Meade Elementary School
Philadelphia, PA
Grades 1-4

As I expected, taking a year to explore the local environment in North Philadelphia with my students presented both challenges and rewards. These stemmed from the fact that focusing on place seemed to break down tidy categories—between curricular areas, between school and community, and between what I knew as a teacher and what I knew and observed as a human being. It was probably the latter phenomenon, the fusion of my professional knowledge with daily experience and observations of nature in the city, that made the year so invigorating.

Under the broad theme Science and Stories in Our Neighborhood, I chose three overlapping perspectives or areas to focus our explorations: Maps, Changes in the Land, and Characters of Our Neighborhood. It proved to be a very flexible framework, able to absorb new discoveries and shift directions as the year progressed. It was also adaptable across the grade levels (one through four) of the three classes I worked with.

We started our study of maps by having a wide-ranging discussion about the children's community: what they knew about it and what its features might be. Everyone participated very enthusiastically—even a few children who were typically reticent—perhaps because they were the experts on this subject. One great surprise to me was the difficulty the students had in coming up with a name for their neighborhood. The closest approximation they proposed was "North Philadelphia." But North Philadelphia is vast, much larger than the area that feeds the Meade School. Since many of them had not experienced much beyond the borders of their immediate community, I had thought they surely had a name for it. But I discovered that because they never had the opportunity to step outside the neighborhood, they had never objectified it or named it. In the brainstorming session the children named many of the community's obvious physical and social components, such as people, cars, shelters (for the homeless, for instance), churches, "Chinese" stores (corner groceries owned by Korean immigrants), and so on. Some children mentioned parts of nature, often generically, like grass, trees, and flowers. Fewer noted specific animals, typically birds or insects. Only one said "nature" broadly.

With the younger children, we followed the brainstorming by making two drawings on 8.5 x 11-inch paper. One was titled "The Place Where I Live"—a simple mental map—and the other, "My Special Place." The older children, a class of third and fourth graders, drew "mental maps" on larger paper, which tended to be a little more complex. Interesting in their own right for what the children chose to show and not to show, and for variations in style and content, these pictures were also a good benchmark for comparison with maps drawn at the end of the year. It was helpful for me to draw my own maps (of my neighborhood) while the children were working, so we could talk about the differences.

A great resource for mapping activities are the large neighborhood property maps made by the city's planning commission, which I found available inexpensively at an architectural reproduction shop. Using these, we moved from discussing basic concepts of distance, scale, and direction, to exploring neighborhood boundaries, and noting the differences between the children's mental maps and these property maps.

I introduced the next map as a mystery for the students to decipher. Each student received a copy of a map that depicted Native American settlements, traditional dwellings, clearings, crop plantings, forests, and native wildlife. The many streams and rivers shown were identified by their Native American names. The children looked first for what

kind of information the map had, what it told about the place
and the people who lived there. Then I asked if they would like
to visit this place—and proceeded to tell them that it was a
map of their neighborhood. The children's incredulity was audi-
ble. That disclosure launched us into discussions about how and
why places change appearance over time, and about the factors
that led to our neighborhood's present appearance. Even the
fourth graders had trouble guessing what might have happened
to the streams that were so conspicuous on the earlier map.

To illustrate how places can change, we read William
Jaspersohn's book *How the Forest Grew* (Mulberry Books,
1992). The book looks at a piece of abandoned farmland as it
changes to meadow and then into forested land—the opposite
sequence to what we had witnessed in our neighborhood
maps. Besides offering a great picture of long-term natural
processes like reversion and succession, the book also served as
a wonderful introduction to many individual "characters" in
our eastern deciduous forest.

By this time, we had started to weave the three themes of
our unit together: maps (and ways of imagining our neighborhood), changes (forest to farmland to city, farm to meadow to

forest, and greening our
own community), and
characters (noteworthy,
unusual, or otherwise
memorable plants, ani-
mals, or people in our
community).

We had already
been using timelines to
note events and changes
in the students' lives, and
changes in geological

time, and now we applied the timeline to neighborhood
changes and events, too. One gap of information in our neighborhood timeline was the recent past. Fortunately, we were able
to attract a speaker who had grown up in the neighborhood in
the 1930s and now works on community development issues.
Floyd Alston also happens to be the current president of the

School Board of Philadelphia, and was happy to be invited to speak at an elementary school. His stories of times past ranged from the prices of movies and candy to descriptions of daily life. He spoke of walking to Fairmount Park (Philadelphia's large forested park) to get fresh, drinkable spring water; of the chores that children were given in those days, like scrubbing the marble steps in front of their houses; of the personal safety that was greater not only in this neighborhood, but everywhere.

> **Meadowland seemed very foreign to the children, since the closest thing to it in their neighborhoods are empty lots.**

Because he is involved with community development—as president of the local community-development corporation, he allocated money to construct the wonderful teaching garden at our school three years ago—he was able to sketch some pictures of the possible futures for the neighborhood, as well.

A few weeks later the landscape architect who designed the teaching garden visited our classes. John Collins spoke about his own reasons for wanting to build the garden and explained the processes involved. He also pointed out a number of the characters in the garden, like the shadbush, which was in full bloom at the time. Collins is a noteworthy character himself, dedicated to using native flora in his work, and trying to integrate a respect for nature into his urban designs. He shared another project that he has been working on for twenty years, which has now entered the construction phase. The Schuylkill River Park will turn a sliver of old industrial wasteland on the edge of Center City Philadelphia into a park of riverside trails connecting the city to the Fairmount Park system. We welcomed the chance to see a piece of land in the process of change, so we scheduled a field trip to walk through this work-in-progress.

To give the children an idea of what their neighborhood may have looked like in earlier times, and to see another example of land in transition, we also took a field trip to a nature preserve. One of a number of preserves in the Philadelphia area managed by a regional land conservancy,

Hildacy Farm was full of characters that we could not have seen in our urban environment. Among many interesting discoveries, the children were especially excited to find owl pellets from a great horned owl, fox tracks, and large pieces of mica. Some of the land is forested and the rest is maintained as meadows. Meadowland seemed very foreign to the children, since the closest thing to it in their neighborhood are the empty lots, which are too full of litter to allow free exploration. Andrea, a third grader, could not resist the temptation to bask in the warm March sun when we reached the upper meadow. "My own private heaven!" she quietly exclaimed. Among the preserve's plants, which are almost entirely native, we saw a grove of familiar foreigners, the princess trees (*Paulownia tomentosa*).

We also made sure not to overlook the nature still to be found in the city, both on the streets and in the teaching garden. We spent several classes throughout the year looking, sketching, and making notes about the characters we found and the changes we observed. A few times when the weather was inclement, we had to bring our subjects indoors. We all observed and sketched the pods and seeds of local princess trees, and then planted the seeds to see what would happen. The germination rate was phenomenal. One of the classes decided to take their seedlings home as Mother's Day gifts. Another class wanted to add them to their tree laboratory, hoping to have full-grown street trees in a few years.

This year's experience confirmed for me the educational value of explorations of place—especially of the children's own neighborhood. It was a pleasure to share with other teachers how such a project could engage children, instill a sense of wonder, integrate subjects, and still meet the national standards being implemented across the district. For me personally, it was a great excuse to develop or practice some of the skills and tools not typically associated with teaching—like my own sketching, journaling, or photography. Finally, the project showed me that place-based explorations can help to revitalize both the school community and the community at large, by reconnecting people to the natural world and to each other in creative and deeply thoughtful ways.

Looking for Changes

Grades: 1-4

Objectives:
1.) To allow children to contextualize the appearance of their community;
2.) To show children how land and landscapes can change in fast and slow ways, by the action of people or nature;
3.) To introduce some plant and animal "characters" of the eastern woodlands;
4.) To show that a forest is a community of such organisms, not just "a bunch of trees."

Materials:
Copies (paperback) of William Jaspersohn's book, *How the Forest Grew*, preferably one for each student.

Time needed:
At least two class periods for reading and discussion of the book; several more for extension activities.

Description:
How the Forest Grew chronicles the changes that take place on an abandoned farm in New Hampshire over a 200-year span. In the descriptive prose and clear line drawings, readers will see the succession of plants and animals that move in, replace the crops and each other, and change the entire appearance of the land. It is a wonderful book to introduce these concepts to a fairly wide range of ages. I have used the book with children younger than the suggested reading level, adapting the text as I read it aloud; the strength of the illustrations helps make this work.

Before reading, ask questions about what your students know about forests: How do they get to where they are? Who plants them? What is a forest, exactly? What kinds of things would you find there?

It is also a good idea to stop at different points throughout the book to reflect on the changes that have taken place thus far, to sum up the plot together, and to make predictions. For instance, what will happen to a field of corn after the farmer and his family move away? How? Peeking ahead in the book is not allowed!

Many good reading skills come into play with this book, too. For instance, one can look for clues in the text that will help young people come to understand what a bobolink or goldenrod is.

After getting through the book, make sure you take time to review and see how close the students' interim predictions were to the ending in the book. Review the kinds of changes presented in the story: What was fast? Slow? How did animals help change the land? How did one change lead to another? Who planted the plants? What was the most surprising thing in the book?

If the class did nothing more than read the book and perhaps write about it, they still would have gained a good amount of new information. But stopping there would be a shame, because it is so easy to extend and employ that knowledge by getting out into the field.

FOLLOW-UP ACTIVITIES:
Mini-field trip: In any neighborhood on any clement day, children can look for succession processes happening not too far from their own homes and schools. In our urban neighborhood, weeds abound in lots where buildings have fallen or been torn down. Downtown, you might have to look harder for weeds, but they can be found.

How many kinds can you find/collect?

Can you find clues about what brought them here (wind, water, animals, etc.)?

In the book, the white pines were the first to grow over the weedy meadow. What are the pioneer trees in your neighborhood?

Finally, based on the story, what do the children think would happen to a particular piece of land—the schoolyard if it is grassy, or an empty lot—if nobody interfered with it for a long, long time? A good writing assignment might ask whether the children would want a forest in their community, if it has none.

Timelines: This book also lends itself to looking at ways information can be presented. You can make timelines about the changes and characters in this book, either as a class project or individually.

Characters: Make lists of the plants and animals that appear in the book. See how many live in your area. Or, start your own chart of weeds, trees, mammals, birds, etc., that you see while making observations in the field or even out the window.

Development: If you live in a developed area, try to locate a map of the area when it was undeveloped, or multiple maps, showing various stages. Talk about development and how those changes may be different (in scale, scope, rate, etc.) from the changes that took place in the book.

Make your own book: Finally, you may want to write and illustrate an overview of how your own community changed, including all the interesting characters you have discovered.

A Place to Begin: Encouraging Community and Sense of Self in the Interdisciplinary Classroom

by Kurt Caswell

The Orme School
Mayer, AZ
Grades 9-12

The Orme School is a community of students, teachers, and ranchers located halfway between Flagstaff and Phoenix, Arizona, off Interstate 17. The school is surrounded by the 30,000-acre Orme Ranch and the Prescott National Forest. When the Orme family bought this ranch in 1929, they opened a one-room schoolhouse for their children and the children of their ranch hands. The school grew as neighboring ranches began to send their children to the Orme Ranch school. Today, the Orme School is an independent boarding school with 185 students, grades seven to twelve. It has changed dramatically in the last sixty years, but the surrounding landscape is largely the same. In all four directions lies horizon, edged with a soft arc of Arizona sky.

During the spring semester of 1997, I taught an interdisciplinary course in nature writing and the literature of arid landscapes with support from The Orion Society's Stories in the Land fellowship program. One of the early guest speakers to visit the course was Orme Ranch manager Diana Kessler. Seated in a circle on the east bank of Ash Creek, twelve students and I heard Kessler talk about her connection to the land. She began by asking each of us to say our names, followed by something about our own connection to this high-desert grassland in which we live. When freshman Aaron Delgrolice asked for clarification, Kessler explained that she wanted him to talk about how he interacted with landscape, physically and spiritually.

"What do you mean?" he said. "I don't interact with the land."

Kessler looked at me and said, "I guess we'll have to

begin at the beginning."

And so we did.

Aaron's response to Kessler's question does not represent a loss or stripping away of human relationships to landscape, but the absence of one to begin with. This young man had so few experiences in nature, he could not even understand the question. Our primary goal, then, was to encourage students to form personal bonds with the land in which they lived, in order to strengthen their sense of self and community and to develop in each of them an environmental ethic. To achieve this goal we needed a knowledge of the human and natural history of the land, opportunities for authentic experiences in nature, and ways of synthesizing our experiences with what we learned.

We built a foundation of local knowledge by reading literature across a number of genres. *Ceremony*, a novel by Native American writer Leslie Marmon Silko, taught us that as the world changes, individuals and cultures must change with it to survive. We used our field guide to flora and fauna, *The Nature of Arizona*, to practice what Edward Abbey preaches in his journal-based nonfiction book *Desert Solitaire*: that physical and spiritual bonds with nature are formed through direct personal experiences. Poems and personal essays from the Spring 1995 issue of *Orion* Magazine, "The Place Where You Live," offered positive testimony to a life rooted in place. And Barry Lopez's collection of short stories *Desert Notes* taught us to listen to the land.

As the weather warmed, we often held class outside. Behind the Orme School chapel, we gathered a number of downed cottonwood limbs into a circle. Here we could sit together in the sun reading and discussing literature. Each of us selected a private place in the vicinity, and sometimes before, sometimes after, our discussions, we would retire to our places and respond to new ideas in our journals.

Journal writing was central to Stories in the Land. During the first week of class, we drove forty-five miles to Prescott to buy our journals. The opportunity to choose their own journal gave the students a sense of pride and ownership in that per-

sonal writing space. We used the journal not only for responding to literature but also for writing stories and poems, recording the events of our daily lives, and sketching and describing
the plants and animals that shared our place. Some days we followed specific journal assignments, and other days we would
sit quietly by ourselves and write whatever came to mind. This
freedom was intimidating for some students, and they had difficulty getting started. So we created a wall chart from a 4 x 4-
foot aerial photograph of the ranch and school, and logged on
it the dates and times of sunrise and sunset, and the phases of
the moon. The practice of recording these statistics with every
journal entry, along with the current time and location, and
notes on weather, gave students a reliable place to begin.
Though repetitive, it got their pens moving, and the words
flowed out from there.

   With a growing foundation in the human and natural history of our place, we began to spend more class time on the
land. Prescott College agroecology student Antonio Massella
often led short walks, on which he helped us to understand
arid ecosystems and identify local plant and animal species. In
late February we walked up Ash Creek to learn about riparian
areas. As we made our way upcreek, Massella knelt near a
patch of last year's silver leaf nightshade (*Solanum elaeagnifoli-
um*). He took a handful of earth and inhaled the sweet, musty
scent. When he encouraged the students to do the same, they
hesitated, then refused. But as Massella told them the story of
the soil and its life-giving properties, one student knelt and
brought a handful of earth to his nose. The rest of the class followed. This student was Aaron Delgrolice.

   On April 8, we took half a day and drove out to the
Sinaguan Rendezvous, a long basalt dike overlooking Little
Ash Creek. The site is awash in petroglyphs, some dating back
to 800 A.D. Orme School counselor and anthropology teacher
Jim Reed explained that Sinagua and Hohokam people came
here to trade, find marriage partners, and celebrate their lives.
After Reed showed us around the site, we assembled in a nat-
ural amphitheater where people must have gathered long ago.
Reed told us that when he camped here, he sat quietly as the
sun fell away into dusk and listened to the stones tell their sto-

ries. "But hearing these stories has more to do with you," he said, "and less to do with the stones." Then we took up our journals and dispersed quietly like seeds to listen for stories from the past.

As the semester progressed, our community grew. In addition to leading outings, Massella joined class discussions three times a week. Following his wife, Diana, Alan Kessler gave a slide presentation on the operation of the ranch. The Kesslers were so interested in our class, they began to read the literature with us. When we invited Yavapai College professor Donn Rawlings to talk about his friendship with Edward Abbey, the Kesslers came to listen. And when photographer Jay Dusard presented landscape and portrait photographs from his books *Open Country* and *The North American Cowboy: A Portrait*, the Kesslers brought their two sons Jigger and J.B.

On April 14, award-winning natural-history writer and illustrator Ann Zwinger came to teach a workshop. That evening we held an informal coffeehouse, an open forum for sharing poems, stories, essays, and artwork. In attendance were some thirty Orme School students, including the members of the course; the Kessler family; Donn Rawlings and Jay Dusard; conservation writer Dr. Dennis Brownridge; singer and songwriter Brooke Adams; English department chair Suzanne Forrester, and another Orion Society teaching fellow, Valerie Sloane, from Orcas Island, Washington. After Zwinger

read a selection from her book *Downcanyon*, students and guests shared their own work. As I sat listening to the many voices telling their stories, I realized that a sense of community arises naturally among people working toward common goals. Here was a room full of people who came together to celebrate each other, and our growing bond with the earth.

Final projects provided an opportunity to synthesize what we had learned with what we experienced. The students were charged with creating a "book." The book might be a broadside, a box, an accordion fold, a mobile, or any suitable structure they could imagine. Four weeks before the project was due, the students began submitting poems, stories, and essays for review. After choosing one or more pieces from this pool of work, they began working on the visual and physical expression of the selected writing. During the last week of school, the students presented their projects to the class. The results were impressively beautiful. Clea Hall-Smith created an accordion-fold book with poems arranged seasonally and accompanied by photographs and illustrations. Joe Martinez created a traditional book structure around his essay about a summer at Aspen Ranch. Michelle Henderson wrote a four-stanza poem on a block of wood that spun round in a framework depicting the seasons. And Marvin Cheuk wrote a series of love poems on fans, nested in a box and scented with dry rose petals.

On the final day of class, we planted six cottonwood trees (*Populus fremontii*) at the entrance to the school. As I moved from group to group, I noticed how well the students worked together, and how their faces held looks, not of hesitation, but of fascination and discovery. I thought then that, as a teacher, the single most powerful tool I have in helping to heal the fractured relationship between people and nature is simply to guide students in their classroom studies and provide opportunities for authentic experiences on the land. The combination of these two key elements will help students define themselves in the context of their communities and the natural world. In trying to reawaken the human spirit to a better way of living on earth, this is a good place to begin.

Book Making

GRADES: 9-12

OBJECTIVE:
To synthesize classroom learning with outdoor experiences through both literary and visual expression.

MATERIALS:
Materials will be determined by individual projects, but could include general book-making supplies such as: cover stock, construction paper, papers of various colors and weights, glue, scissors, paints and brushes, colored pencils, needles, and book-binding thread. Other supplies might include: word-processing computer, heavy cardboard, small cardboard boxes, lumber scraps, basic woodworking tools, dried flowers, leaves, and grasses. Ambitious classes may want to try making their own paper.

TIME NEEDED:
One to four weeks, depending on other class activities taking place during the project.

DESCRIPTION:
Step 1: Teacher presents project providing sample book structures and visual examples. Include photographs from books on bookmaking, or make samples of a range of book structures such as: traditional books, broadsides, accordion folds, mobiles, and books from boxes. Encourage students to be creative, but caution them against a project that requires rare and expensive materials. Simple structures are often the most beautiful. By taking photographs or collecting donated finished projects, the teacher can build a project library to present to future classes.

Step 2: Students collect three to five pieces of their own writing (poems, stories, essays) to choose from. Encourage writing that details personal understanding and experiences in nature. The writing does not have to be long but should be powerful.

One good poem is better than three sloppy pages. If students want to create a collection of work, encourage them to choose related pieces, so that the book structure will be meaningful to each piece. Individual consultation with the teacher may help students select meaningful pieces for their books.

Step 3: Students begin to revise writing and develop book structures. Insist on a structure that makes sense for the nature of the writing. The writing and the physical book should work together, so that each is an expression of the other. Often working with scraps of paper and glue to create models will help students formalize their plans. In some cases it may be easier to choose writing that fits a particular structure rather than develop a structure around the writing.

Step 4: Students continue to revise writing with peer groups and/or teacher, while collecting materials to complete the book. Teacher may be of great aid in helping students to find materials, drawing on both school resources and local art supply stores.

Step 5: Students submit final draft of writing to teacher for review and final revision.

Step 6: Students create book.

FOLLOW-UP ACTIVITIES:
Students present books to classmates and/or community. They describe book structure, relationship between the writing and the book, process of construction, and read selections from the writing. Books might also be displayed in a library or trophy case.

Exploring Nature: Science and English in Conversation
by Jennifer Danish

The Peddie School
Hightstown, NJ
Grade 8

After a few years of living and teaching in Hightstown, New Jersey, at the Peddie School, I had come to the quick conclusion that this place was not beautiful. Only an eighth of a mile from the New Jersey Turnpike, Peddie sits on almost one hundred acres of land, some of which is forest and lake. But one can always hear the roar of the highway. There are no hills or open valleys. Each field and farm in the area is surrounded by fast-breeding houses and business developments. Although the Peddie School campus itself is beautiful and well kept and green, it has no surrounding mountain vistas, no clear brooks rambling around its borders, and no fields of green that are not mowed every forty-eight hours.

Popular distaste for the New Jersey landscape is nonetheless what inspired my colleague in the science department, Kim Zanelli, and me to develop a course for eighth graders that would explore their surroundings. We hoped that by linking science and English through an exploration of the land, we might better connect our students to their place—a landscape that is so easily dismissed as damaged beyond repair.

While it may be rewarding to take students to the places in their world that are wild and magical, this task becomes challenging in a landscape that is developed and not particularly postcard-beautiful. Our course would need to develop our students' power of observation so that they would be open to seeing wonders of their landscape not visible from a car or an athletic field. New Jersey's flat plains and arteries of roads would push us to look beyond the human spaces and into the woods and wilds that require more work and patience. We would have to build a connection to the land over time and through discoveries made day by day.

The premise of our interdisciplinary course "Exploring Nature: Science and English in Conversation," was the importance of observation. As Rachel Carson writes in her book *A Sense of Wonder*, "If facts are the seeds that later produce knowledge and wisdom, then the emotions and impressions are the fertile soil in which the seeds of knowledge must grow." When students can take the facts of the scientific world and experience them through their senses, these facts become infused with emotional meaning. We hoped that our students would use the lenses of science and English to better understand and see the land, and therefore build a greater connection to it.

> **We built our curriculum like a story that could develop and grow as the year progressed.**

We were able to implement this kind of integrated learning because we convinced our school of its potential value. Not only did we have the assistance of an Orion Society Stories in the Land fellowship, we also had the approval of our departments and the academic dean. When a school supports an interdisciplinary program both philosophically and institutionally, it creates more room for teachers to explore the possibilities of integration. We were given a ninety-minute block each day to meet with all twenty-four of Peddie's eighth graders. While we might do more science or more English on any day of the week, we were free to make those decisions as the course evolved and were not constrained by our subjects. The course curriculum became centered not simply on content and knowledge but on skills and attitudes as we tried to consider what we wanted our eighth graders to be like, as scientists and writers, by the end of the year.

We built our curriculum like a story that could develop and grow as the year progressed. Because Peddie divides the year into trimesters, we centered the themes of the curriculum around three different ideas.

Developing observation skills was the central theme of our fall term. We began by asking our students the question,

"Where Am I?" The initial assignment asked them to map the Peddie campus. We did not give them much guidance, hoping that they would undergo a process of orienting themselves to the land. We kept their completed maps for two months and handed them back when we began a unit on topography. The students were amazed at their first attempts to draw the campus because they realized there was so much about the place that they had not seen as newcomers. As we continued our study of maps and their meaning, the students' maps of the school became more detailed and elaborate.

Our next step in teaching the techniques of mapping was to take our students to a part of the campus that is often unexplored and unmapped: the Peddie Woods. Most Peddie students never see this area of the Peddie landscape or places like it in New Jersey. On a warm, damp, overcast morning, our students were presented with the task of mapping the woods by exploring the area and learning its boundaries, variations, and topography. At first the group was apprehensive and overwhelmed by the assignment. The place they were mapping was so foreign to them that learning its details and borders seemed an impossible assignment. As soon as they began to head off into the corners of this world, however, the complaining subsided and the wonder increased. Kim and I enjoyed their sudden discoveries along the way: openings and clearings in the dense vegetation, a bridge leading to the heart of the woods, and even an old bathtub acting as a dam in the creek.

In addition to a map of the

woods, each group was required to prepare a set of directions to a special spot of its choice. Their directions included conventional signals and turns, but also gave evidence of their newly acquired powers of observation. Some had come upon caves and unusual trees that looked like shelters or human figures. Others had found detours and forks in the woods' trails that led to the edge of the creek. They were discovering their own stories in the land even though they had only spent one morning there, and in spite of the fact that there were no familiar brick paths leading them to these destinations.

KEY

Smooth Sumac =
Downy Serviceberry =
Scarlet Oak =
Pachysandra =
Birch =
Elm =
Other Large Foliage =
Other Small Foliage =
Snake Hole = .S
Rabbit Hole = .CB
Trail =
Bridge =
Plank =
Grass =
Paved Road =
Dirt Road/Path =

The legends on their maps revealed that the students had noticed more than the obvious. One girl included a symbol of a car horn to mark the places in the woods where you could hear cars on the New Jersey Turnpike. Her legend revealed not only the swamp-maple grove and the bends in the creek that feeds the Peddie Lake but the human intrusions as well. By exploring the details of this semiwild place, our students discovered its natural beauty and the places where it had been shaped by human influence. Their maps of the woods revealed that they were beginning to see and observe the world around them with more sensitivity to the interactions between humans and nature.

The winter term took us to the heavens with a study of astronomy and mythology. Another skill we wanted to foster in this course was public speaking and teaching. We devised a winter project in which groups of students were each assigned a different constellation and tasked with learning about it from a number of angles. In presentations, the groups explained the brightness and distance of the major stars as well as the mythology behind the constellation's name.

In the early weeks of the spring term we became eager to return to earth and the habitats and bioregions of New Jersey. As the land thawed, we anticipated the chance to spend time

ALEX KAUFMANN

in the field. We decided to take our students away from Peddie to Blairstown, New Jersey, where we could study the habitat and natural history of an area very different from our own. Having witnessed our students struggling to get along together in the bleak month of February, we hoped that this trip would give them an opportunity to relate to one another outside the bounds of the school's walls. Before leaving, the class met to talk about fears and expectations, and almost every student voiced apprehension about traveling with classmates to a wild place. They feared not getting along and growing bored in a place far from the comfortable routine of their lives at school.

The minute we arrived our students seemed to be transformed. Just a few miles from the Delaware Water Gap, Camp Mason is a northern-forest habitat, rich in comparison to the inner-coastal plain from which we had come. On our first day, we participated in a low ropes course and climbed a twenty-five-foot climbing tower. What had been causing strife in our classroom world was now falling away as the students concentrated on moving one another through seemingly impossible physical challenges. They were learning the principles of community and teamwork in a place far removed from their suburban world.

As the three-day experience progressed, our students frolicked together and stole moments in the woods around the cabin to write in their journals or look for signs of spring. On walks with our guides, we came to see that the natural history of the area was rich with stories. A forest dotted with stone walls revealed an agrarian past where farmers had cleared huge trees and rocks in order to grow crops. Standing in the dense oak and hemlock, one student marveled at the fact that farming had once prevailed here. Back in Hightstown, the primeval forest has not been allowed to come back because its rich soil continues to be farmed for crops.

On our second day, we left for a hike up Catfish Mountain, the tallest mountain in the area. The beginning of the hike led us by a beaver dam that was changing the forest into pond before our eyes. One student remarked that she had seen humans change the land to create homes and comfort, but never an animal. We reached a natural spring and refilled water bottles, another first for many of our students. The group

was intrigued by the water's origins and its purity, and they
wondered about the source of their own water at home.

By the time we reached the summit of Catfish Mountain,
the skies had turned gray and March winds were whipping at
our faces. Nevertheless, some of the group nestled against rocks
to take in the view while others climbed the fire tower to enjoy
a larger vista. We heard more than one student comment that it
was the most beautiful view they had ever seen, even with gray
skies and a frozen landscape.

Their feelings of accomplishment increased when it began
to snow and we were suddenly in a rush to get back to the
camp. The adventure of weather and wilderness kept them
busily talking all the way down the trail. We observed an
immediate transformation in the land. The next morning we
asked our students to take fifteen minutes in the cabin to write
down their reflections and observations. They wrote furiously
and silently, demonstrating that they had absorbed some
important experiences. We knew this trip had been powerful
when we read this journal entry:

> I have never been alone in the woods with my
> friends able to do whatever I want....You cannot
> know this feeling until you have seen the vast
> acres of pine. When I looked to the ground, I did
> not see trash, instead I saw pine needles and
> maple leaves covering the rich soil. Even though
> the leaves were dead, I could still see a spark of
> life in them, a spark that cannot be found in a
> city or a town, but only in a forest. It was the
> effects of the silence, the way you could see tree
> after tree, it seemed as if the scenery would never
> end. All I could smell was the pine and no pollu-
> tion. Now, I don't just think of the outdoors as
> bugs and mud, I think of the beauty and the
> freedom of the landscape.

We returned from Camp Mason with a transformed group.

Because one of the major goals of our course was to
encourage our students to become stewards of the land, we were

delighted with the opportunity to invite a first-grade class from Trenton to our campus. Each first grader was paired up with one or two eighth-grade "buddies." Before they arrived on campus, their teacher, Jill Casey, arranged a letter exchange between buddies. When the first letters arrived, complete with drawings, our students were shocked and thrilled by the naiveté of the first graders. Their buddies wrote that they were afraid of seeing wolves and bears in the Peddie Woods, that they wanted to bring frogs and ducks home with them, and that they wanted to catch rabbits. The eighth graders waited for their first graders to arrive with anxious anticipation. Each eighth grader developed a lesson plan for his or her hour-and-fifteen-minute class, and some students brought in visual aids and other materials to better teach their buddies about nature.

When the eighth graders took their buddies out into the Peddie Woods and to its surrounding lake, we saw awe in the eyes of the first graders. Our students were showing them ducks, fiddleheads, lily pads, red maple trees, and crab-apple blossoms. They pointed out poison ivy and explained its dangers. They swung from Virginia creeper vines and made leaf rubbings of oak, maple, and birch trees. With the use of homemade puzzle pieces, they learned about food webs and the interdependence of living organisms. We were amazed by all that our students taught their younger buddies. Everyone was engaged and extremely excited about sharing the natural world. We were rendered speechless. As the day progressed, we watched our students embody the meaning of stewardship. They had instilled the wonder of the landscape they had come to know so well into the minds of these first graders, many of whom rarely see an open field.

Our year culminated in the production of a student environmental magazine that chronicled lessons learned about the land during the course of the year. The magazine project incorporated many of the skills we had developed throughout the year: observation, descriptive, personal narrative writing, creative presentation, and group work. We were taking a number of risks with this project—for start, we did not know how to use the technology our students would need to create the magazine. From the beginning, this was a student-centered endeavor. Everyone in the group had a stake in making the magazine work and everyone had to learn and teach each other new information. By the end of the project, our students had become editors, artists, and publishers of their own work. When *Nature Speaks: Listen* was finally back from the printer, the class marveled at what they had been able to accomplish.

As I look toward teaching in the twenty-first century, it strikes me that my students will need the skills to use the technology of the computer age. They will need to learn how to manage the maze of information that is available to them through the internet. But I also know from my experience teaching this course that my students will need to know how to observe the natural world around them. Watching them connect to the land has shown me that this must be at the heart of my teaching in the future. In a world that continues to grow faster and more complex, the simple act of walking through a wooded area to see the change of seasons and understand the trees and flowers that are characteristic of a particular region opens the possibility of developing a lifelong connection to a place. Our students need to be able to look closely and carefully at the world around them and see the wonder that lies within nature. It is easy to become spoiled by fast electronic images and to forget the calls of birds and the names of the flowers that bloom where we live. But as teachers, we have the opportunity to take our students to the inner regions of the land we dwell upon and invite them to discover the possibility that awaits them.

Creating an Environmental Magazine

GRADES: 9–12

OBJECTIVES:
1.) To display student writing and artwork from the year in a magazine by using the latest computer technology;
2.) To create a medium for student environmental writing that would inform and educate the rest of our school;
3.) To help students gain skills in group and teamwork through a two-month project;
4.) To teach students the skills of editing, production and layout, art/photography editing, and the fundamentals of desktop publishing.

MATERIALS:
Student writing taken from the year pertaining to the themes of the land and the local bioregion.
Adobe PageMaker or a comparable desktop-publishing program.
Laser scanner for artwork and photography.
Access to a local printer who can work with a camera-ready proof for a reasonable fee.

TIME NEEDED:
A full semester (three months) or a whole year if the curriculum will allow it.

DESCRIPTION:
Early in our planning of this course, my partner, Kim, and I hoped that our final project of the year would be a student-produced environmental magazine. We wanted the magazine to chronicle the lessons students had learned and observations of the land that they had made throughout the year. As spring approached, we began to share our ideas with the class. Because we were taking an off-campus trip early in the term, we hoped to use some of that time to begin planning our magazine.

Our first step in producing the magazine was to develop a list of jobs and duties that needed to be filled before we could begin. After reading some descriptions of these jobs, each student applied for a position on one of four different staffs: art and photography, editing, layout and production, and circulation and printing. We asked the students to explain why they were interested in the position and what they could offer to the staff. We read each proposal and then made decisions about where to place everyone. Then we began to meet for part of each week to discuss preliminary plans. What did we want our pages to look like? How would we go about editing the writing? We looked at copies of *Orion* and *Wild Earth* for ideas about layout and design.

Students met in their respective staffs and began the brainstorming process. Jennifer Sahn from The Orion Society visited our class one day to talk about how *Orion* Magazine is produced. She came with an armful of magazines and spoke about the publishing process. She walked students from the beginning of an issue through to the end, explaining some of the detailed steps that they might not have otherwise known. After her visit, we found that the class was more focused on their own vision for their magazine.

Our students had been writing about their bioregion, environmental issues in New Jersey, and our class trip to the northern part of the state. We asked each student to submit the two pieces they were most proud of. It was then time for the editors to begin reading and editing the submitted work. In their first meeting, we encouraged them to develop criteria and a scoring system for each essay. These would help them make decisions about which pieces they wanted to publish and why. After many tries, they created a system that they were happy with and divided up the essays for a first read.

Meanwhile, the production staff began experimenting and learning how to use our Pagemaker program. We asked students from the yearbook and newspaper staffs to come in and give our production staff a few tutorials. They began experimenting with various templates and design ideas. Soon, they were teaching each other new tricks and shortcuts on the program. We asked them to report to the class on a few of their layout ideas. They also drew on a blackboard a master plan or pagination for the magazine, listing where each article would eventually fall and what artwork might go along with it.

Eventually, the editors began to return essays to the authors. They told each author which of his or her pieces they liked best and made suggestions for readying them for publication. The writers made revisions and submitted them on a disk to the editors who had read and commented on their writing. The editors read through each piece again, making cosmetic changes, and then posted them onto our computer network so that they could be imported into the Pagemaker program by the production staff.

When the essays were in the network and a final list of articles had been decided upon, the art and photography staff was given a tentative table of contents and copies of the articles. They began to create drawings and sketches to go with each of the pieces. We also scanned clip-art and photographs that students had taken during the course of the year. We learned from the circulation and printing staff that we could print our magazine more cheaply if all of the images were scanned and downloaded into our publishing program. This would be the final step for the art and photography staff.

I still remember the elation the class felt when the first article and photograph were placed into the program. The magazine was developing before their eyes and everyone had an integral role in its future. A boy in the class who had not had a particularly positive experience during the year had his article placed first. He could hardly contain his joy on seeing his title and byline.

NATURE SPEAKS : LISTEN

Pia Aklian

ALEX KAUFMANN / PIA AKLIAN

Just before production week, we had a class meeting to select a title for the magazine. We wrote a number of nominations on the board and talked about what we thought were central themes in the articles that would be published. Everyone became very passionate about the various options for titles, but we finally managed to narrow our choices to two. When the final vote was a tie, Kim and I cast both of our votes for *Nature Speaks: Listen*. Many of the students in the class were upset that we had been able to vote. They exclaimed that it was their magazine and we should not have an opportunity to vote on the title. At first, we were surprised by their reaction. In retrospect, we couldn't think of a more positive outcome. They felt so much pride of ownership in the magazine that they didn't want us meddling in their final product.

The selection of a title was just the beginning of our magazine craziness. With three days left in our production week, we had only twelve pages laid out and thirty-six still to go. We weren't sure it could be done. It was Friday, the magazine was due to the printer on Monday morning, and we thought we had blown it. One week wasn't enough time for production and we knew that. However, the kids decided it was going to get done. Groups of them signed up to come in on Friday evening, Saturday afternoon, and all day Sunday. We provided the snacks, and they did all the work. After over twenty-one hours of work, we were ready for final edits on Monday morning. Kim and I each edited a couple of the pieces, but the students did most of the editing.

When we looked back over our experience with the magazine, we realized that our students had become the stewards of their own project. We all learned about how to produce a magazine, and this allowed Kim and myself to be mere supervisors and directors. When the final deadline was upon us, it was the kids who decided to work extra hours and make it happen. In their final self-evaluations, many of them said that it would have been productive to make the magazine a year-long project. They also felt that the experience had taught them skills they might not have learned otherwise. They enjoyed the challenge of such an extensive project. When Kim and I reflected on this experience, we realized how little we had known before starting the project. It was perhaps the best risk we have ever taken as educators.

Monterey Bay: A Sanctuary of Promise

By Bonnie Dankert

Santa Cruz High School
Santa Cruz, CA
Grade 11

A few years back, I volunteered as a staff member to "shadow" a high school junior, for the purpose of experiencing "a day in the life of a student." Traveling from class to class, following the student's daily routine, I took copious notes from the blackboard, observed each teacher's style and format, and absorbed the lessons intended to foster student success. At the end of the day, I was exhausted—drained from hours of listening, but grateful for some very valuable insights. Virtually no effort was being made to give practical relevancy to the subjects; no subject was tied to issues in the community; and no attention was given to the declining capacities of the world's natural systems or to the cultural patterns that will, in the long term, threaten our very existence.

Today's culture exerts tremendous influence on a student's motivation and goals. Daily experience is centered on a consumer-oriented, technology-based lifestyle. Responsibility is informed by self-interest, while the individual maintains a friendly indifference toward the larger world. Generally speaking, students at Santa Cruz High School do not see themselves as valued by their community. To them, "community" translates to physical location. The connection between sharing and storing knowledge and the health and vitality of the community is seldom mentioned, except for brief reminiscing about the catastrophic 1989 earthquake. At school, ecological citizenship is limited to a small enclave of "tree-huggers" who roam the campus promoting and taking responsibility for a school-wide recycling program.

So in 1995, when I was awarded an Orion Society fellowship and initiated a place-based study of the Monterey Bay, I set off on a challenging journey. I wanted students to feel less alone, and I wanted to promote a relationship with, if not stewardship for, our place on the Pacific coast. I also hoped to use this study to address some of the larger cultural and environmental issues of our time. In *The Unsettling of America*, Wendell Berry reminds us, "The definitive relationships in the universe are not competitive but interdependent.... We can build one system only with another. At certain critical points these systems have to conform with one another or destroy one another." Thus, it becomes evident that the deepest foundations of human life are rooted in the well-being of ecosystems. In order to avoid the destruction Mr. Berry foresaw, we must foster and develop active ecological citizenship in all of our schools. This process must be seen as a critical component of the curriculum, connecting schools and teachers to the wealth of resources found within their local community.

At the start of our Monterey Bay study, some of my students thought our state's history began with the arrival of the Spanish missionaries. Yet indigenous California was once one of the most culturally diverse regions in the world. The Ohlone Indians' ancient history dates back over 10,000 years. To better teach the depth and complexities of the Ohlone culture, I contacted the Natural History Museum of Santa Cruz, hoping to arrange a visit to their Ohlone exhibit. When Docent Coordinator Doug Petersen heard about the Monterey Bay Studies course, he invited my entire class to participate in an upcoming docent training session on Ohlone culture. The training was held at a 3,000-year-old Ohlone site containing bedrock mortars and ancient rock art etched in lichen-covered walls along a peaceful, hidden creek. Two Ohlone women, Linda Yamane and Jackie Kehl, met us at the site, neither of whom had seen the native art before.

JINJING ZHANG

Our group spent the morning preparing and sampling a buffet of Ohlone foods. We served ourselves chia seeds, pine nuts, miner's lettuce, elk jerky, smoked salmon, and manzanita cider. In addition, we cooked the Ohlones' most significant food staple, acorn mush, the traditional way by introducing red-hot rocks into a functional cooking basket woven from redbud and willow shoots, bear grass, maiden-hair fern stems, and sedge roots. The leached acorn flour, water, and chia seeds heated to a rapid boil. Soon a thick soup was ready to be eaten. It was challenging for students to imagine this as a daily diet, but I compared it to the mornings when my mother prepared a hot dish of Cream of Wheat for my brother and me before sending us off into the snow for school. We discussed our reading of Malcolm Margolin's book, *The Ohlone Way* with Linda and Jackie, noting their personal insights regarding Margolin's written portrayal of their culture. In retrospect, one of the most memorable moments of the course was being with these two Ohlone descendants as they discovered part of their cultural legacy.

> **The process of developing active ecological citizenship in all of our schools must be seen as a critical component of the curriculum.**

Not far from this site is an area covered with live oaks, where John Steinbeck was born and raised in the small town of Salinas. The geology and coastal climate of "Steinbeck Country" no doubt inspired his detailed descriptions of the flora and fauna of our region. I introduced the geological and tectonic dynamics of central California in layman's terms and supplied a watershed map illustrating the stream canyons and rivers that empty into Monterey Bay. Those of us living west of the San Andreas Fault, from San Luis Obispo to Montara, live on what is known as the "Salinian Block," a part of the earth's crust that was formed 200 miles south and has moved to its present location over the last thirty million years. Hiking along the wind-swept beach with sketchbooks in hand, my students and I explored Natural Bridges State Park, where we sat on bedrock outcrops to discuss plate tectonics.

Later in the quarter, we conducted a tidepool study with Dr. John Pearce, professor emeritus of biology at the University of California at Santa Cruz. Tidepools are thriving ocean communities located along a seam in the intertidal zone and are known to be some of the most biologically productive ecosystems on the planet. Before going to the edge of the sea, we visited the university's Long Marine Lab, where aquaria house a large selection of the marine creatures found in the Monterey Bay. We were fascinated with the colorful spectrum of invertebrates—purple, pink, and orange—that drift on the tides from the moment of fertilization. Then there were the sea snails, shrimp, crabs, gribblies, and worms that wriggle in cracks and crevices.

As we were escorted to Dr. Pearce's research area, the smell of sea air rushed toward us. We were reminded of the sights and smells of Doc's Western Biological Laboratory described in Steinbeck's novels *Cannery Row* and *Sweet Thursday.* My students were surprised to learn about Edward F. Ricketts, one of Steinbeck's closest friends, and the marine biologist upon whom the character Doc is based. Like Ed Ricketts, John Pearce is a born naturalist as well as a scientist. Dressed in rubber boots, a windbreaker, and worn jeans, he knelt down on slippery rock wet from seaweed to share with us his fascination with the intertidal zone. His smile and enthusiasm were contagious.

We rolled up our sleeves and went to work, trying to identify and describe what we saw. Students were firing questions as fast as Pearce could answer them. One student discovered a baby octopus in a nearby pool and the group rushed over to look. John gently placed it in a clear container of sea water, and some of us attempted to depict this incredible creature in detail in our sketchbooks. Recollecting what we had learned from two visiting university students enrolled in the science illustration program, we added field marks, making sure all data we

JINJING ZHANG

recorded could later be used
for identification purposes.

The following day, we
read Rachel Carson's chapter "The Rocky Shore" and
used her writing as a model
for reflective narratives
about our previous day's field study: "True understanding
demands intuitive comprehension of the whole life of a creature...how it survives amid storms and surf, what are its enemies,
how it finds its food and reproduces its kind and what are its
relations to the particular sea world in which it lives." I encouraged students to do additional research in the library to better
understand the organisms they had sketched, learning as many
details about their topic as possible before beginning to write. I
supplied field guides and reference books to inform our narratives. When the pieces were complete, we read them aloud.

We spent a full day visiting the old Horden Cannery,
remodeled in 1982 to become the world-renowned Monterey
Bay Aquarium. This educational facility recreates what a diver
would actually see beneath the moving swells. Students added
a stratum to their understanding of the bay by viewing a fea-
ture-length video about the bioluminescent creatures swim-
ming in the dark depths of the bay's remarkable submarine
canyon. We stared in disbelief as we watched creatures that
looked like pulsating prisms swim slowly by the eye of the
camera. These images made a lasting impression, reminding us
of how little we know about our oceans.

Down the street from the aquarium, we visited Cannery
Row, noting the changes that have taken place since
Steinbeck's days in the 1940s, when the overharvesting of sar-
dines caused the canneries to close. La Ida's Cafe and Brothel is
now Halisha's Restaurant. Lee Chongs market is The Old
General Store. The only original structure is Ed Ricketts's old
laboratory at 800 Cannery Row. Outside it, on a wooden construction fence, is a nostalgic mural of Cannery Row painted
by Bruce Ariss. We walked amid the tourists and passed by
novelty shops and small restaurants to find a place where we
could huddle out of the wind to eat our lunches.

The next day we held class outdoors and created a large-scale, 20 x 25-foot map of Monterey Bay, using a grid-map system and water-based paint. Students indicated key geographic locations and points of interest. We used a stepladder to get a bird's-eye view of our map and search for errors.

Back on the beach, we observed the western snowy plover,

a small threatened shore bird whose nesting season coincides with the time humans most love to spend at the beach. Plovers create their nests in the sand by the male wriggling his belly to make a depression. The nest is sometimes marked or camouflaged with shells, rocks, and twigs. The inconspicuous speckled eggs of plovers are easily missed and trampled by people running or walking across the beach. When adults detect a predator, they flee the nest and leave their incubating eggs, which then may be buried or blown away by the wind. People may unknowingly cause harm if they are unaware of the plover's habits. Through studying the plover's situation, we came to realize that our actions and decisions have an enormous impact on the ecosystems around us, and that it is up to us as individuals to decide how we want to treat this place called home.

When my students and I look out onto the bay now, we visualize the diverse habitats and marine life living just underneath its surface and at the interface between water and land. We have come to understand that the Monterey Bay, designated a national sanctuary in 1992, remains largely unexplored, much the way our country's mountains and deserts were 100 years ago. As students, teachers, and citizens, we need to seriously commit to the long-term conservation, restoration, and preservation of our country's ocean frontiers.

Not only did our relationship with the bay grow over the course of the year, but we did too. We became a "community" and enriched ourselves during the process. We shared laughter, travel, and food; we told stories of beauty and loss. We learned together where our drinking water comes from, how beaches are formed, and observed and studied the animal and plant life that share our place. Our time in the field inspired dozens of illustrations and photographs of resident cormorants, gulls, sea otters, harbor seals, sea lions, synchronized schools of slender fish, and giant kelp, the plantlike algae that functions as an underwater forest for sustenance and protection of marine life.

Creating an interdisciplinary study relating to where we live on this coast allowed me to challenge my students with nothing less than the real world around us—a world that has been compromised by destructive habits, inattention, and complacency. I demonstrated to students how disciplines overlap and integrate. It is time schools come to see the direct connection between work confined to the classroom and the complicity of the educational establishment in creating a passive or even "hopeless" generation. We must not be afraid to move beyond the widely accepted canon of traditional texts and mandated curricula to develop grade level standards and skills that can be articulated and achieved through any course of study. If schools do mirror the values of society, we need to further address our own thinking about the ecological crisis we are in. We need to share solutions and change our ways.

Make a Place Map in Your Schoolyard

GRADES: 6–12

OBJECTIVE:
Students will use math, art, and geography skills to produce a
scale map of their home region on their school blacktop using
a grid-map system, chalk, and paint.

MATERIALS:
Multiple copies of a scaled map of your home region or
watershed
Broom and dustpan
Compass
Three quarts of water-based deck paint: blue, green, and brown
White chalk
A chalk line (a tool for drawing straight lines available at hard-
ware stores)
Measuring tape
Stepladder
Paint brushes
Several clean, empty tin cans or milk cartons
Plastic tub or bucket of soapy water
Damp rags, sponges, and paper towels

TIME NEEDED:
4–5 hours

DESCRIPTION:
Find or trace a simple line map of your region or watershed,
including geologic features like rivers and mountains and
names of nearby towns and cities (for my class we mapped the
Monterey Bay Sanctuary). Reduce or enlarge your map to fit
in a rectangle measuring 8" x 10". Form a grid over your map
by dividing it into 2 boxes and assign a number to each box.
(Your grid will be 4 boxes by 5 boxes—a total of 20.) Make
copies for distribution and prepare other materials for the
mapmaking activity.

Select a location on the blacktop for the map. Choose a smooth cement or asphalt area that is at least 20' x 25'. Have your students sweep the area clean of debris and dirt. Find the north compass point and determine the appropriate direction for your map. Using the chalk line, snap a straight line 20' long at the left-hand edge of your map. At each end of that line, snap a 16' line running to the right, perpendicular to the first line. Then, snap a straight, 20' line to complete the rectangle.

Next, measure and mark each side of the rectangle into 4-foot segments. Connect the marks on opposite sides of the rectangle to create a grid that is proportionally equal to the one on your map handout: 5 boxes long and 4 boxes wide. Using the chalk, number the 20 squares on the grid to correspond to the numbers on the scaled map. In the bottom left-hand box, draw a small compass and identify N, E, S, and W.

One nice thing about this activity is that you can get a variety of people on campus to help. I like to involve parents, campus supervisors, janitors, and maintenance people—even some of the clerical staff, if they have any spare minutes. Assign groups to each numbered square to reproduce in chalk on the blacktop what they see in the corresponding square on the map handout. Groups working on adjacent squares will need to make sure that their drawings align properly at the edges. When the chalk map outline is done, use the stepladder to gain a bird's-eye view of the map and correct any errors.

4'x4'			
1	2	3	4
5	6	7	8
9	10	11	12
13	14	15	16
17	18	19	20

Then have groups paint along the chalk lines and paint in the names of geologic features and place names, including the location of your school. Depending on the number of people, you can add significant detail to the map (we added creeks and rivers, the lighthouse, state parks, favorite surf spots, the gray whale migration path, and the elephant seal rookery). You can also identify sites that your class has studied or visited. You may want to invite participants to add their favorite places in the region or watershed to the map as well.

I like to ask students to note the open space or agricultural land along the coast. In our region, it is important for students to recognize how this land is being used and how it impacts the bay. The majority of my students have no history of the grassroots efforts to keep these places available for their enjoyment. I stress that the greenbelt surrounding the city of Santa Cruz did not just happen and strive to help them realize their own obligations to protect and enjoy this coast.

The schoolyard map is ambitious but fun! And it can be a community-building activity as well. Creating a map of the region out in the schoolyard seems to just draw people in. It's like baking batches of cookies in the kitchen—the next thing you know, there's folks standing around telling stories and eating cookies. The entire school community will learn from the map as it comes together.

(Adapted from the Los Marineros Program developed by Diane Heidemann and Jerry Chiu.)

Treasuring the Tetons
by Jo Anne W. Kay

Tetonia Elementary School
Tetonia, ID
Grade 5

A spider, dropping down from a twig
Unwinds a thread of her devising
A thin premeditated rig
To use in rising.

And all the journey down through space
In cool descent and loyal-hearted
She builds a ladder to the place
From when she started.

Thus, I, gone forth as spiders do
In spider's web a truth discerning
Attach one silken thread to you
For my returning.

Perhaps E. B. White best captured the essence of acquiring a sense of place in his poem "Natural History." The silken threads he describes lend meaning and endearment to life's adventures.

Teachers hold a key to that binding process, for we have the ability to teach children to cherish and understand the earth. Although our communities may be vastly different, our financial resources limited or nonexistent, we all have the ability to bring experiences with the land into the classroom, and to help our students develop "silken threads" of awareness and knowledge that will bind them to their places.

The Orion Society offered me the means to pursue this adventure through its Stories in the Land fellowship program and enabled me to see that place-based education is not only feasible, but an essential part of my fifth-grade curriculum. My task was to help my students acquire the knowledge, emotion, and sensitivity that would enable them to treasure the history and heritage and beauty of the place in which they live. I would attempt to weave those threads of connection throughout the entire school year. And in doing so, I had one of the most rewarding teaching experiences of my career.

To understand our valley, we first had to learn about its human beginnings. This subject lent itself very nicely to the required fifth-grade study of Native Americans. Contact with a local university put me in touch with a wonderful outreach program through which an expert in local Native American culture visited our classroom for an entire day.

What a treat that day was! Students traced the migration of Native Americans into our valley, learned about early tools, clothing, transportation, and food, experienced eating pemmican, learned to throw an atlatl, and listened to Native American folk tales. This visit coincided with the beginning of a year-long writing project as students were starting to keep their own journals. The students retold folk tales and wrote essays on what they had learned during the day. Art was a natural outcome of the visit, and during the subsequent weeks we created Indian weavings, pottery, and masks.

Since winter comes early to our valley, we took advantage of the weather in early September for our first field study. "A Day in the Canyon" was planned for all the fifth-grade classes in our school district. With the help of the Teton Valley Land Trust, a local volunteer organization, students spent the entire day in a natural classroom. The volunteers manned stations on stream life, wildlife, folk stories, botany, nature drawing, and hiking. Students rotated through the stations collecting samples that we brought back to the classroom and used to set up mini-ecosystems for observation. Journal entries for that day reflected the students' feelings as they experienced nature:

RACHEL WOOLLEY

Treasure Mountain
By Sheena Knight

Treasure Mountain
Reminds me of
Experiences in the woods
And cool air and
Sunshine.
Usually I take bigger
Routes, but this one was still
Excellent.

Mountains
Ought to be climbed
Unless a person is
Not capable.
Try, try, try,
Are the words used
in climbing, and
Never giving up.

Treasure Mountain
By Kristin Kaufman

My experience at Treasure Mountain was amaz-
ingly wonderful. It was amazing because of the
things I learned.

I learned that when you look and feel things like
trees, you can tell what kind of tree it is. For
example: you can tell a fir from a spruce because
a fir has flat, soft needles, and a spruce has square,
spiky needles. A pine tree has sharp needles that
split into two needles. Lodgepole pines have needles and branches further up the tree stump.

As the year progressed, student journals began to fill with
wonderful poetry and prose. Students read local papers and

collected clippings of history, environmental issues, weather, and other special interest features that pertained to Teton Valley. We shared the articles as a class and then copied them so that each student could add a copy to his or her journal.

One of the areas of focus for my project was bringing members of the community into my classroom as well as taking my students to places in the community where they could learn the heritage of the land. Any time you invite the community into your classroom there is a moment of panic as you question whether they will be able to relate to your students and use the time wisely. As I contacted older members of the community to visit my class, that sense of panic was soon put to rest. Each person I invited was more than happy to share their expertise and spend time with my students. They brought their own personalities into the classroom, and my students were very receptive to their visits. Our class learned about archaeology, bridges, post offices, historical figures, agriculture, Native Americans, early schools, and endangered species from these local residents. Students learned firsthand that the older members of the community can make a valuable contribution to their education.

Applying these locally focused educational experiences to the year's curriculum added a new and vital dimension to my teaching. Writing assignments that had been a drudgery for many fifth graders took on new meaning as they wrote about things they had learned from members of the community who visited our class. Students learned how to take notes, ask relevant questions, and ask for clarifications so that they could write pieces that reflected the accurate history of our valley. Visitors were amazed at the attention they received from ten year olds.

> **Sharing our discoveries of the world around us was opening up areas of our hearts and minds that a sterile classroom experience couldn't touch.**

Inspired by Marcel Proust's statement, "The real voyage of discovery consists not in seeking new landscapes, but in having new eyes," I attempted to help my students acquire a new perspective on their home through the use of the camera. Students paired up and chose a theme for their photo experience. Themes varied from agriculture to wildlife, from forms of transportation to historical buildings. Each group was given a camera to record their observations using twenty-four pictures. Each student chose his or her favorite photo to be enlarged to 11" x 14" and framed. All the photos would be added to their journals.

The class took their photo project very seriously. One spring day on my way to school, I spotted a flock of sandhill cranes feeding in a field about a mile from school. I hurried to school to find the students who were covering the theme of wildlife. A quick trip was made back to the site so that they could capture the early morning scene.

Something magical was happening in my classroom. The silken threads were attaching the children to the land, but also, like a spider's web, the threads were attaching the children to each other and especially to me. Sharing our individual discoveries of the world around us was opening up areas of our hearts and minds that a sterile classroom experience couldn't touch. The threads of common purpose were also binding the children to their parents as they shared the experiences of our project at home and sought out information about how their family had come to live in the valley.

We shared two novels during the winter months, *Jenny of the Tetons* and *Expedition Yellowstone*. We also started writing to teachers at the Teton Science School who would be coming to our class in the spring and sharing two full days on the Teton River with us. Students wrote letters to these pen pals telling them about themselves and about the books we were reading. Letters came back over the mountain with drawings and pictures. As we finished *Expedition Yellowstone*, the students created a crayon transfer quilt showing scenes from Yellowstone. Each student drew a scene from the novel with crayon. These drawings were then transferred to cloth by pressing with a hot iron, and the pieces were sewn together and quilted.

In February we spent a full day in Jackson Hole visiting the National Wildlife Art Museum and the National Elk Refuge. The class was thrilled to actually ride in horse-drawn wagons right out among the elk herd. For many, this was their first experience with large game animals.

When spring arrived, the group from the Teton Science School came to class, and students met their pen pals, who now became their group leaders as they experienced the river. On the first day, students investigated wildlife and stream life, and came upon what looked like an old trapper's camp, complete with writing materials and other items a fur trapper might have carried. The class was excited to find that the camp was just like the ones described in *Expedition Yellowstone*. On the second day, students were taught how to conduct water-quality tests on the river water.

Back in the classroom, we decided to create sculptures of five of the most common animals in the valley: elk, moose, bear, badger, and coyote. This was a huge project, but once again, the community provided an expert artist who came to class and helped the students with proportions. Soon animal figures were emerging from chicken wire and papier-mâché.

As a final activity, each student created a book titled *Teton Valley from A to Z*. As a class, we brainstormed each letter of the alphabet for words that related to our study of Teton Valley. With a master list in hand, each student developed a personalized picture book of Teton Valley.

All too soon, it was the end of May, and photo projects, journals, quilts, and sculptures were complete and ready to share. Students created a wonderful display in the gymnasium to which they invited the other classes in the school. Each of my students was assigned a group to take through the exhibit while sharing stories of the experiences of the year. The following day, parents and community members were invited to view the exhibit. My students summarized their year in many different ways:

I have learned a lot this year. When I first moved here, I thought it was a boring place. But now that I've come to fifth grade, I've learned how important the land, plants, animals, and especially the wetlands are. I used to litter, thinking it wouldn't hurt the land, but I learned that if garbage destroys the wetland, it won't come back.

J.C. Hoopes

This past year in fifth grade, I've learned to respect the Valley more. When we were taking pictures, I realized all the things that we have and should take care of. If you were going to be in this class this past year, you would have learned a bunch of stuff like about all the stories and water—everything.

Brian Wade

So, though the year was over, the project endured. Hopefully, my students took with them more than bulging journals and art projects to collect dust in some long-forgotten treasure box. Hopefully, the real treasure had become part of them, and they, too, would come to treasure the Tetons.

A Day on the River

GRADES: 4-6

OBJECTIVE:
Students will gain a greater understanding and appreciation for their natural surroundings as they learn more about the major river in their watershed. They will learn to conduct scientific experiments, collect data, and write conclusions about their findings.

STUDENT MATERIALS:
warm clothes
hiking shoes
sack lunch
rain gear

CLASSROOM MATERIALS:
Individual zip-lock bags for each student containing sample bottles, magnifying glass, tape measure, pencil, small notebook.

STATION MATERIALS:
straining screens (4)
thermometers (4)
large plastic containers (1 per group)
chemicals and materials for pH-balance testing, phosphate testing, and bacteria testing
field guides for birds and mammals
art paper
art pencils
drawing boards

TIME NEEDED: one full school day

DESCRIPTION:
One of the best ways to teach about nature is to go out into nature. Get your students out of the classroom for a day on the river (or in some other area of interest in your community).

The key to success will be securing volunteer help from community members.

A Day on the River has become a tradition for my students. They look forward to spending an entire school day outdoors. With a good staff of volunteers, your day will run smoothly and you will be able to enjoy the activities too.

Well ahead of the day, schedule volunteers to help with the following five stations:

Water life: At this station, students will learn about watersheds and their importance to a good water supply. They will test the river water for temperature, pH balance, phosphates, and bacteria. You will need responsible adults to help with this activity since chemicals are needed to conduct the experiments. Students will also fill a clear plastic container with river water and add specimens from the river to take back to the classroom for observation.

Wildlife: At this station, students will learn about some of the most common animals that live in the area around the river. They will look for signs of these animals and learn how to identify prints and bird calls. If the river has a beach area, casts can be made of bird and animal prints. This station is also a good place to learn about food chains and interdependence.

River history: Local story-tellers can use this station to tell stories about the history of your area. They should be prepared to tell about the importance of the river to the development of the community and changes that have occurred in the river over the years.

Nature hike: Hiking through the wooded area or meadows surrounding the river will add to the day. Students can identify trees, plants, and undergrowth, collect specimens for the class-

room, and stop to do journal writing along the way. This is a
great time to learn to identify native plants.

Nature drawing: To really observe an object it is ideal to see it
in its natural state. At this station, students spend time selecting
plants or trees in the area to draw. They might also use the
materials near the river to create nature sculptures, working
individually or in groups of three or four.

When the day is over, gather your class together to share
impressions of what they have seen and heard during their
experience on the river. Back at school, students should be
sure to leave their specimens and ecosystems in the classroom
so they may use them the following day.

FOLLOW-UP ACTIVITIES:
Poetry writing: Nature makes a great subject for poetry and children will be eager to write about what they have experienced.

Research: Have students choose one subject in nature that they
learned about and do a research report to learn more about it.

Art: The nature drawings that students began in the field can
be refined and final copies made on heavy art paper for display.
Flowers and plant specimens can be pressed and used for
bookmarks.

Ecosystems: The large plastic containers that the students have
brought back to class with water and land materials can be
arranged and placed where students can observe them over the
coming week. Live specimens collected by the students the day
before can be added, but covers should be used to contain them.

SUGGESTED READING:
Nature All Year Long, by Clare Walker Leslie. New York:
Greenwillow Books, 1991.
Nature Drawing: A Tool for Learning, by Clare Walker Leslie.
Dubuque, IA: Kendall/Hunt Publishing, 1994.

Opening the Door for Young Naturalists

by Daniel Kriesberg

Locust Valley Elementary School
Bayville, NY
Grade 4

I wanted them to know this year was going to be different right from the start. On the first day of school, as soon as all the children were in their seats, before anything else, I took them outside. Our year began outdoors and ended outdoors. In between we were very busy. My goal was to combat what Robert Michael Pyle calls "the extinction of experience." I told my students we were going to learn about their place by going out and exploring. I wanted them to gain a greater sense of wonder, joy, knowledge, and reverence for the natural world. If nothing else, my students and I were going to *experience the outdoors.*

With the support of The Orion Society, I was able to purchase ten day packs and fill them with a variety of tools to help children explore outdoors. Each pack contained magnifying glasses, a pair of binoculars, field guides, a compass, a sketch pad, a journal, and a camera. Every time we took a trip we brought our packs. Not surprisingly, the children loved having all that equipment at their disposal. The packs helped us get to know our neighbors.

Over the course of the year we took more than ten trips to local natural areas, concentrating most of our time in Shu Swamp. On each trip we took time to sketch, write in our journals, and sit silently. I allowed the children unstructured time to explore with their naturalist packs, in addition to more formal activities. This was always my greatest conflict: freedom versus control. Time was short. I wanted to give the children a lot of freedom to explore and learn on their own. I also felt the pressure of teaching something, helping my students to be productive. "How can you just let children hang out and run around in the woods doing nothing?" Did I really trust the value of time spent exploring on their own? I had my own agenda, but there was this other agenda out there set by the rest of the world.

Back in the classroom and schoolyard, I tried to integrate our experiences throughout the curriculum. I wanted to model for the other teachers that environmental education does not have to be a separate subject taught by nature experts. We spent time on basic ecological concepts that concluded with the children inventing an animal that is adapted to the schoolyard. A hands-on study of crayfish helped make the concepts come truly alive. Whenever possible I taught a math lesson outside, such as estimating plant populations, finding tree heights, and making scale drawings. The trips helped make our study of geography and Native Americans more realistic, and social studies became part of this study in a variety of ways. They saw an isthmus firsthand, they drew lots of maps, and tried to make stone tools and wigwams in a forest. The students began to see how geologic history, natural history, and human history are entwined.

> I wanted to model for the other teachers that environmental education does not have to be a separate subject taught by nature experts.

Each child picked one of the animals that lives in Shu Swamp and researched and wrote a report about that animal. In art they made acrylic paintings of their animals. On May 8, 1997 we put up these reports and paintings in a display case at the information kiosk at Shu Swamp. There was a short ceremony with the preserve manager and many parents in attendance. A local TV station even filmed a segment on the project for the nightly news. The children were thrilled to see a long-term project come to a successful end. Afterwards we took a walk searching for spring wildflowers. It was truly a special day.

One important skill I learned this year is public relations. With just a little effort I was able to get my class and their work in the news several times. Not only is this a thrill for the children but it helps promote the goals we are all working for. I simply called our local papers and television station, told them about what we were doing, and wrote up an explanation.

We wrote a lot of poetry inspired by the journal writing we did on the trips. Another source of ideas were the many incredible picture books we read over the course of the year. For open house night, each child made a poster with captions using photographs taken over the course of the year. Some children combined poetry and drawings with their posters.

In the schoolyard we made a tree trail with a cassette-tape tour identifying the schoolyard trees. Each teacher in the school was given a copy of the cassette tape. We celebrated the completion of the trail by planting white pine seedlings.

I was also able to find fourteen puppets representing our local wildlife, and the children wrote short puppet shows for the second-grade classes.

In June, I pretended to be an amusement-park developer who wanted to buy Shu Swamp. The children role-played townspeople deciding what to do with the land. This was a chance for them to show me what they had learned, to express their feelings about the place, and to rehearse the kinds of decisions they would make as adults.

Parents were involved and supportive of the program. The trick is to get more of them involved. When they came on a

trip or saw the class in action they were impressed. The children tended to report back only the fun stuff: "Mr. K. climbed on a tree upside down." They didn't keep their parents up to date on things like grammar lessons. I want the parents to realize how educational these outdoor experiences are and how they link the curriculum together. In order to achieve that, I need to do a better job of communicating exactly what happens when we go afield.

Next year I plan to take the program another step. I want to integrate the study of place into even more of the curriculum and hope to involve more parents in our work. I was awarded a grant from a local teacher's organization and will use the money to buy more naturalist packs and other equipment. We will do an in-depth study of the arboretum across the street from the school. We will focus on this place and through it tell Long Island's story. The project will take all

year and cross all curriculum areas, resulting in a book called *The Natural and Human History of Long Island*, which we can sell to raise money for the following year.

I have also been awarded a grant from the School Parent's Association to build a nature trail behind our school. Once I had an overall philosophy and plan for the coming year I found it easier than expected to find more grant money. Funders were interested in supporting a project that had a solid base and incorporated innovative ideas.

It is always hard to measure the success of an educational program. It is easy to get distracted by the demands of report cards, disciplining students, getting through the required curriculum. When I think back over the year I remember small signs that signal success: a student nervously asking if he can take a naturalist pack home to use in his backyard; overhearing two boys plan a way to come back to Shu Swamp to play hide and seek; watching a child sit by a stream and write nonstop for twenty minutes and still complain when I tell everyone it is time to go; the way fear and disgust changed to excitement when we searched for pond creatures; all the seeds, leaves, galls, and insects that keep coming into our classroom each morning.

As teachers we need to have realistic goals. Not every teacher is going to jump on the bandwagon. I would be kidding myself if I claimed that these children have all become connected to the outdoors. Children come to our classes with ideas and preconceived notions about life. Connecting to the natural world has to begin at a young age when children still talk to animals. Like the people restoring the tallgrass prairies, we can only try to restore their natural sense of connection to the outdoor world one patch at a time. I am reminded of Mrs. MacFarland, my third-grade teacher. I did a project for her on birds. Every Sunday I cut out the weekly article on birds from the *Syracuse Herald Journal*. I kept track of the birds that came to my feeder and checked them off in my brand-new Golden Guide. I have no memory of writing a report or reading encyclopedias. I do remember the bird feeder I made. If I trace my lifelong interest in nature to the beginning, that's where it starts. We show our students the door, give them a chance to go out and explore. Some will stay, and that's what counts.

Young Naturalist Journals

GRADES: 2–6

OBJECTIVE:
To help young writers pay better attention to the world around them. Good writers lead awake lives. They notice the world. Keeping a nature journal helps children walk with their eyes open to the world and to their feelings. Children can experiment, take chances, and be honest in their journals. Our role as teachers is to encourage, inspire, prompt, provide opportunities, help, and guide them.

MATERIALS:
Of course each child needs a journal. There are a wide variety of journals to choose from. Since much journal-writing time will be outside, durability is essential. Spiral notebooks usually don't last. Other than that, the choice is wide open. It should be a personal decision. Personally, I like the black-and-white-marbled composition notebooks. You may want to make your own journals with your students.

TIME NEEDED:
Do regular journaling exercises throughout the study.

DESCRIPTION:
Virtually all of our most famous and influential naturalists kept journals. Journals are a way to live moments in life over again. Journals preserve certain moments and make them special. Journals are a chance to reflect, question, wonder, scream and yell. It is a place to be sad or happy. Journals listen to whatever we write. Journals can make the everyday magic. A random thought or an interesting observation takes on an added importance when recorded in a journal. Journals help children realize that their thoughts matter, are worth recording. They do not have to have something "important" to say. The entries in their journals will be the ingredients for poetry, stories, essays, and reports. A nature journal becomes the history of the place

and of the person. The journal is firsthand research. The journal is a gift for the future, a window to the past.

The beginning of the year is the time to start a nature journal. The skills the children will learn will be important all year. There are many ways to set up a journal-writing program in your class. It can be daily, weekly, monthly, or saved for trips to local natural areas. It is important to make it a habit. Regular journal writing becomes a ritual and emphasizes its importance. There can even be a class journal with different entries each week by different students.

Writing should be done in the outdoors as much as possible. Direct contact with the outdoors makes the writing vivid. Encourage children to write with detail and reflection. A journal is more than an account of the day's events. Journals are not limited to words. They can be places to sketch, paste in pictures, photographs, feathers, pressed flowers, and other items that have meaning. You don't have to be a nature expert or go to the mountains to have a nature journal. The outdoor world is such a fascinating subject that a schoolyard is a place of wonder.

If it is possible to take the children on a walk to a natural area there are even more writing opportunities. Taking a class on a nature walk is not as hard as it sounds. Within walking distance from your classroom there may be a park, arboretum, nature preserve—even a cemetery or vacant lot. A few trees on the playground are worth a visit as well. If you are going far afield, bring extra adult supervision and make your behavioral expectations clear to the students.

Model the way you keep a journal by sharing some of your own journal entries and the thought process you go through when journal writing.

Entries should be dated and nothing should be thrown out. One line can be just as important as twenty lines. Read passages from other journal writers. Collect good journal entries from students as a benchmark to give children a better idea of the standards you expect and the level they can achieve. Continue to model and share journal entries throughout the year to maintain high quality.

I divide the journal entries into three categories. Over the year the students experience a mix of these:

Free writing: Free writing is exactly that—free writing. I give the children time to write whatever they want.

Suggested entries: I use these when I want a little more focus from the students. Sometimes I let them choose from various prompts. Some children prefer to have suggestions. The main thing is to get them to write about their place. Here are some possible prompts, in no particular order:

• What would you show someone if you took them on a walk through this place?
• How is your mood affected by this place?
• Imagine being in the place a whole year. What are its rhythms and patterns?
• How does this place compare to a place you dislike?
• Is this the kind of place you like? What kind of places do you like?
• What has changed since last time we were here? (Have them observe seasonal changes.)

Assigned entries: Any of these prompts can become an assigned question. Assigning journal entries is a good way to do a quick evaluation of an activity or find out what the class is thinking. They are also helpful if everyone has given the same question some thought for class discussion. If you decide to read these entries on a regular basis, you have the chance to write back and have more interaction with the children.

Lean toward the freedom side rather than the structured side when giving journal-writing time. The overall goal is to help students become lifelong observers and journal writers. The journal has to be the child's choice, their place to write without worry. An occasional required assignment is fine. Some children will not produce much when given freedom. Others will use it to the fullest and shine more than if you required everyone to always do the same thing.

RESOURCES:
A Book of Your Own: Keeping a Diary or Journal, by Carla Stevens. New York: Clarion Books, 1993.

A Gathering of Days, by Joan Blos. New York: Atheneum, 1980.

Into the Deep Forest, by Jim Murphy, illustrated by Kate Kiesler. New York: Clarion Books, 1995.

Night Letters, by Palmyra LoManaco, illustrated by Normand Chatier. New York: E. P. Dutton, 1996.

Sarah's Questions, by Harriet Ziefert, illustrated by Susan Bonners. New York: Lorthrop, Lee and Shepard, 1984.

A Writer, M. B. Goffstein. New York: Harper and Row, 1984.

Wetland Wisdom

by JoAnn Kruzshak and Debbie Levy

Thetford Elementary School
Thetford, VT
Grades 1-4

Walk down the primary corridor at Thetford Elementary School and you will see a hundred pairs of little boots, in various colors of the rainbow, lined up along the walls. Each day of the week, children put on their boots, grab their clipboards, and march purposefully across the village green and down the road to a nearby wetland, where they participate in a year-long ecological study. Thetford teachers have been lucky to be able to use this ecologically rich and diverse three-acre wetland as a classroom for three years, and we were excited to expand and deepen our wetland study project as part of Stories in the Land during the 1996-97 school year.

Our project was centered around weekly visits to the wetland, which were introduced and followed-up by activities in the classroom. Before school began, we attended to procedural matters, setting up liability insurance through the school and asking permission of the landowners whose properties we were to use. Each class chose a day of the week as its "wetland day" for the year. Parents were notified of our plan and asked to make sure their children had proper clothing and boots for the excursions.

For two weeks before we ventured out to the wetland, we worked extensively with our students on safe field-trip behavior. This was especially important because we would walk along a busy road to reach the wetland and would be around water once there. We wanted the children to understand that there are rules and boundaries out of doors just as there are in the classroom. To accomplish this, we had the children brainstorm the rules and learn and practice safety signals. At least two adults accompanied each class, and a first-aid kit was always carried. We also taught respect for wetland plants and animals, emphasizing the rule: "Leave the wetland as we found it."

By mid-September we were ready for our first field trip. In the classroom, we introduced a topic by reading stories. For example, *Around the Pond, Who's Been Here*, by Lindsay Barrett George (Greenwillow, 1996), was used to introduce wetland animals and their habitats. Reading stories such as this helped the children focus on the theme of the day's visit. After reading, they discussed animals or sign that they might see at the wetland that day. Then we would review rules and present an overview of the day's activities, drawing maps and showing the route we were to take before embarking upon our journey.

Once at the wetland, we'd all sit on a fallen log and participate in a focusing activity, such as "The Sounds or Color Game," from Joseph Cornell's *Sharing Nature with Children*. This helped the children quiet down from the walk and prepare for the day's work. The activity before us would be reviewed, materials handed out, and small groups of students formed. Our activities ranged from active exploration of the area to games that taught a specific concept, or the observation and recording of natural phenomena through drawing and writing.

Beavers are active in the pond we frequented, so looking for sign was a part of every trip: fallen trees, gnawed branches in the water, and, in winter, holes and trails of bubbles in the ice. Our walk across the ice to explore their lodge was a highlight of the year. Being so close to the lodge enabled the children to use their own senses to learn more about it. And was it smelly! One class spontaneously began building beaver sculptures out of snow. Another played "Oh! Deer!," a game from *Project Wild* that teaches about animal survival rates in winter. At Christmas time we made gifts of food for the wetland animals.

The next part of each visit involved sitting in what we called "magic spots" on the shore overlooking the beaver lodge. Each child chose his or her own spot away from classmates and was expected to sit quietly for five minutes, observing what was happening around the wetland. We'd then gather in a circle to share what each of us had noticed. As the year progressed, the children's observations became more detailed and their ability to sit in silence improved. Sitting quietly to observe nature was a skill that they definitely had to learn, but

as time went on, they began to look forward to spending time in their magic spots.

Each visit to the wetland ended with a story, often a Native American legend, relating to the theme of the visit. We found that reading stories outside was particularly powerful. One day, while we were reading "Koluscap and the Water Monster" from *Keepers of the Earth* by Michael Caduto and Joseph Bruchac, a frog croaked as if on cue, adding a timely sound effect to the story, much to the children's delight.

After returning from wetland visits, children were asked to write and draw in their science journals, an exercise that allowed us to observe their progress in writing throughout the year. These sessions were followed by art projects: making habitat dioramas and seasonal murals, singing songs, drawing, painting, sculpting, and writing poetry.

For one project, students spent several weeks researching the wetland animal of their choice. We instructed them as a group on how to find and organize information, then asked them to write and illustrate their own reports, which were shared with parents and peers. Through the project, the children developed a sense of expertise, and an innocent sense of "ownership" and affection for the animals studied. Some children acted as a resource for their classmates, becoming experts on their particular animal. Often, these "experts" were the children who tended to struggle with other aspects of school. The experience of the project was empowering. The children strongly identified with the animals they studied and often would incorporate that animal's habits or behaviors into their dramatic play.

We often used literature to teach science concepts because it provided a link between science and other areas of the curriculum. To strengthen the relationship between home and school, and to provide our students with different modes of creative expression, we set up "Creature Feature Bags." These were cloth bags, each filled with a stuffed wetland animal, several children's books about that animal, a science, art, or cooking activity, a journal, and helpful hints for parents about reading to and with their child. Children were encouraged to use the journal for writing about their "adventures" with the animal. Some wrote up personal research about the animal; others wrote poems or riddles. The children kept the bags for five days, then shared their journal entries. This was a powerful extension of our science work into the children's homes, and it made our work at school much more meaningful to their families.

Literature was also used as a springboard for the children's own writing and creative expression. For example, we read *Old Home Day* by Donald Hall (Browndeer Press, 1996) during our study of local history. The book describes the settlement patterns and land use over time in a fictional town very much like our own. After several readings, students worked in groups to create murals of our town at different times during its history. To teach pond succession and the effects of beaver activity on the environment, we read *The Beaver Pond* by Alvin Tresselt. The children then drew their own versions of each stage in the sequence of succession. We read aloud several books by Thornton Burgess, such as *At Paddy the Beaver's Pond*, because they contain a wealth of information about animals, and our students loved them.

The success of our experience is hard to measure, as it is primarily based on values. As a staff we came to appreciate the collegial support we provided each other in the wetland study. The joy of purchasing and using new teaching materials was tangible. But most rewarding has been the pleasure we took from watching the students learn about and come to love a special natural place. These students have made a strong and long-lasting connection with the wetland, which will act as a catalyst for further learning. Seeing signs of beaver activity, climbing on the lodge, putting an ear to its surface to hear the sounds coming from inside, smelling the overpowering scents that emanated from within, and making our own lodges out of clay and sticks were powerful personal experiences, ones that could not have been gained from books alone. Learning outdoors in a natural setting, using all their senses, the children absorbed more information. Guided by the multisensory experiences we provided, along with those provided by the wetland itself, the children became active participants in their own learning.

Our difficulties in executing the wetland study were minor, revolving primarily around the vagaries of weather and nature: i.e., a nasty infestation of wasps in autumn and a winter that wouldn't quit. At some times it was necessary to give attention to the children's behavior. For the most part, these problems were related to their excitement over being at the wetland. Teaching safe field-trip behavior at the beginning of the year saved much time and in the long run resulted in a greater appreciation of the experiences we had planned.

In looking back, our work at the wetland has taught us the tremendous value of exploration for its own sake. Giving children the time and freedom necessary to explore the natural world allowed them to develop a set of experiences to which more sophisticated knowledge can be added. It is our hope that by sharing our own experience we will inspire other teachers to consider using a place on or near their school's grounds as a base for teaching and exploration activities.

Creature Feature Bags

GRADES: 1–4

OBJECTIVES:
1.) To strengthen the home-school partnership;
2.) To provide authentic reading/writing activities related to the child's real-life experiences;
3.) To provide opportunities for personal responses to literature;
4.) To integrate imaginative and realistic fiction with personal writing about wetland and forest animals.

MATERIALS:
For a classroom of twenty children we provided five "Creature Feature" bags. Each contained a stuffed animal, four or five fiction and nonfiction books about that animal, a craft, dramatic play, or cooking activity, an audio tape, and suggestions for parents about reading to their children. In addition, each bag had a journal, in which children were to write about their creature.

TIME NEEDED:
The project continued throughout the year. Teacher preparation time was 6 to 8 hours.

DESCRIPTION:
We wanted to provide our six-, seven-, and eight-year-old students with many opportunities to read and write about science. We often used books to introduce a science concept, and developed the Creature Feature Bags as an exciting and appropriate way to strengthen the reading-writing connection. We also wanted to have parents involved in their children's literacy development. Creating a home-school partnership was an important goal of this project.

We applied for and received a grant from the New England Reading Association for $600. Support could also come from a PTO or other fundraising activities. For each classroom of twenty we provided five bags, each filled with a stuffed animal that might call the wetland home, literacy materials, and detailed information for parents about supporting their child's attempts at reading and writing. Suggestions included strategies for questioning, encouraging comments, and ways to help early readers focus on important aspects of the text. The goal was to provide mutually enjoyable literacy experiences for both parent and child. Parents often expressed their appreciation for these suggestions; they spoke about how relaxed their children were when reading, and the pride their children took when they could figure out words independently.

The bags were distributed among the five primary classrooms at the school and rotated on a six-week basis, so that each child took several bags home during the course of the year. They went home on Wednesdays (most classes kept a sign-out schedule) and were due back the following Monday, so that those who forgot them had a day of grace before the next group needed them.

On Tuesday mornings, students shared their adventures with the animals in the bags. They read from their journal entries, which often began a discussion or teaching moment related to the animal or a specific characteristic of the wetland. Children were very creative in their activities with the stuffed animals. Some made clothes for them, or made them beds from found objects. Others made food for their animals, or toys they thought the animal might like to play with. One child wrote a retelling of Goldilocks with his beaver as the main character. Sharing was an important aspect of the Creature Feature Bags, as one child's idea often led another to think of something unique to do when his or her turn came to take the animal home.

TEACHER RESOURCES:
Botany for All Ages, by Jorie Hunken. Old Saybrook, CT: Globe Pequot Press, 1989.
Doing What Scientists Do: Children Learn to Investigate Their World, by Ellen Doris. Portsmouth, NH: Heinemann, 1991.
Exploring the Forest with Grandforest Tree, by JoAnne Dennee and Julia Hand. Montpelier, VT: Foodworks, 1994.
Hands-On Nature: Information and Activities for Exploring the

Environment with Children, by Jenepher Linglebach. Woodstock, VT: Vermont Institute of Natural Science, 1986.

Keepers of the Animals, by Joseph Bruchac and Michael Caduto. Golden, CO: Fulcrum Publishing, 1991.

Keepers of the Earth, by Joseph Bruchac and Michael Caduto. Golden, CO: Fulcrum Publishing, 1989.

Keepers of Life, by Joseph Bruchac and Michael Caduto. Golden, CO: Fulcrum Publishing, 1994.

Tracing Our Culture Back to Its Roots

by Lorain Varela

Pecos High School
Pecos, NM
Grades 9-12

The people of Pecos, New Mexico, and its surrounding areas do not come from a single homogeneous group. Rather, they represent a variety of racial, cultural, and linguistic backgrounds that have come together over the course of history. As an educator in this place, I have found that students learn best when school experiences are related to their personal lives and cultural backgrounds. As they become aware of their cultural legacies, they are able to achieve a clearer, firmer sense of themselves as individuals, and thus better succeed in school and in life.

As a Stories in the Land fellow, I began the year by reminding students in my multicultural English, world, and U.S. history classes how crucial it is to identify with one's cultural background. Because none of us enters the world alone. We are each a complex mixture of where we come from, where we are going, and what we bring along with us. Each one of us is in a continuous state of formation, and we each affect the formation of those around us.

It is my belief that continuity with the student's past must be maintained while alternatives for the future are examined. With the knowledge and freedom to choose among real-life alternatives, the full potential of any person can be realized. While no student learns exclusively in one style, an educator can make learning situations more meaningful by knowing which activities or teaching techniques a particular group of students tends to respond to; more than one means can be used to arrive at the goal. The goal is to teach students to observe, analyze, and evaluate the alternatives available to them. Using a place-based approach as the organizing theme for this inquiry worked for us.

We began with a unit on regional folklore. Students collected and examined local legends that focused on the culture of Hispanic New Mexico. After reading *Cuentos of My Childhood* and *Folklore of Rio Abajo*, which were written in Spanish and English, students went home and interviewed their parents and other relatives. Parents were invited to come to class and tell their own *cuentos* and share their experiences with us. Having parents visit the classroom made the unit more personal, and therefore more meaningful, for the students. At the end of the unit, final reports were written and oral presentations were made to the class.

My students then wrote and illustrated two large-sized books of folk tales from *Cuentos of My Childhood*, which they read aloud to first graders. The first graders did "echo" readings, giving my students a chance to see how reading is taught. In a follow-up to this activity, we discussed how the reader must select what is important, understand it thoroughly, and fix it in his or her memory to succeed in comprehension. Then we moved on to note taking, underlining, and, finally, applying the new ideas in various situations—all from teaching reading to first graders using cuentos and other stories of the region. One of my students who was enrolled as part of the special education inclusion program had been a very poor reader himself, always asking not to be called on. After a couple of trips to the elementary school, he wanted to read, and the younger students actually encouraged him. Watching my students come alive at the elementary school further convinced me that education is more successful when we leave the classroom and find new places and faces.

A poetry unit was then introduced. Each student was asked to write a poem and select a setting where the poem was to be delivered. The local church, cemetery, the *esequia* (ditch), students' cars, and classrooms became the backdrops as students were videotaped reading their poetry. Students loved leaving the classroom and having the opportunity to choose a setting for themselves. John Lucero wrote over thirty poems based on his life as a gang member. He told of his love for his mom, and of ultimately having to choose between the gang and her. Students read his poetry and also did *paño* (handkerchief) art.

When we returned to the classroom, we viewed the video and critiqued each others' poetry. The students were particularly surprised to realize that they themselves could make meaningful contributions through telling their stories. John's poetry even got published in a car magazine. We also collaborated with the elementary school students on the poetry unit. The first graders were doing butterfly art, so my students wrote haiku poetry to describe the butterflies painted by their young friends:

Calm…just a white bloom
but for wafting butterflies:
wild gardenias!

In the multicultural English class, music was used as a means to show how the environment around us is changing. Water and water rights are very much an issue in New Mexico. Results from water-quality tests performed on the Pecos River in 1992 and 1993 indicated heavy levels of PCBs in the fish that inhabit the river. The Forest Service provided my students with a short presentation on the many threatened or contaminated rivers in our state. We also learned how parts of New Mexico are being used as dumping sites for nuclear waste. One group is busy trying to prove that the salt beds in Carlsbad are a safe place for the toxins. Indian casinos are another contribution

to the changing landscape. Students compared pictures from yesterday and today, noticing changes in the land, and coming to terms with the fact that change is inevitable. We composed a song using the tune to "This Land is My Land," which told of the environmental changes that New Mexico is faced with and reminded us that the land is ours to protect.

Guest speakers were brought into the classroom as well. Students would suggest an uncle, mother, or friend of a friend who could help us learn about our culture and our place, and I would try to arrange a visit. While studying China in the world history class, we invited a masseuse to teach us about pressure points. The students got a short demonstration on massage and a short lecture about its history. The classroom was transformed with art from China and Japan. A trip to Santa Fe to eat Chinese food was appreciated as well. Students used chopsticks and noted the decor of the restaurant. They carried on conversations about the history of China with the owner and waitress. They were delighted that studying China did not have to come right out of a textbook. On the way home students asked where we were going next—they didn't mean a trip, they meant what country were we going to be studying. We then went to Rome and Greece, and our classroom was converted into a Roman building, with columns and arches made out of paper and tape. The unit came to a close with a delightful Greek meal prepared by another class visitor.

A unit on local architecture followed and the experience of creating the Roman structure helped students to appreciate the local buildings that surround them. The churches, pueblos, and other structures came alive in their eyes. Our trip to Old Town in Albuquerque was exciting and very educational, as students noticed the influence of early Roman architecture. One student said, "my grandmother's house looked like this and they never went to Rome." When we traveled to Santa Fe, we observed differences in structure and style such as windows, doors, and furniture. We discovered that the famous "Santa Fe style" had really come across the ocean thousands of years ago. A trip to Acoma Pueblo allowed us to muse over its distinct architectural style. My students were impressed by the fact that vigas and adobes, rock, and other materials had been carried all the way to the top of the mesa in order to build the pueblo there.

At year's end we traveled to a local restaurant where we reunited the first graders with high school students for a final celebration. We presented them with the giant books we had made for the reading unit. They still remembered all the characters and even the plots of the stories. "The Rock Cutter" and "How Chili Got Its Name" were their favorites.

The year's study provided my students with new vistas of who they are. They became more aware of the relationships between individuals and their cultural origins. One eleventh-grade student wrote:

> I really love to be on horseback on mountain
> trails in the warm summer sun or when the
> leaves on the trees start to fall. When you come
> to a clearing and see all the valleys below it's a
> beautiful sight. I like the way the wind is soft and
> slow as it makes the tall trees dance and sway. Or
> the sound and feel of your horse stepping on a
> fresh blanket of fallen leaves. I like these places
> because they make you feel like you are in touch
> with nature and away from all of the modern-day
> rush and crowdedness. There are a lot more rea-
> sons that I like these places, but basically they fit
> me and my lifestyle.

Our studies were enriched by the freedom we had to leave the classroom, and to not have to rely on textbooks for learning—even in world history class. Our knowledge of each discipline grew as a result of our research and travels, and we ourselves came to know a bit more about who we are, where we come from, and where we are going.

Experiencing Poetry

GRADES: Adaptable to all grade levels

OBJECTIVES:
Through reading, writing, song, and research, students will become familiar with poetry and how it can bring new meaning to commonplace human activities and experiences.

1) Define poetry;
2) Explore the origins of poetry;
3) Learn different purposes and forms of poetry;
4) Study the poetic form;
5) Write and analyze poems.

MATERIALS :
Paper
Pens/pencils
Poetry anthologies
Video camera
VCR

TIME NEEDED:
2-3 weeks for research, reading, writing, and filming

DESCRIPTION:
Poetry is something secret and pure, some magical perception, lighting up the mind for the moment.

Have students find as many definitions of poetry as they can, through a short research exercise in the library. Ask students to name which poet defined poetry for them and to read a short poem by that author. Discuss the origins of poetry, tracing it back to religious ceremonies. Explain how the poet became the recorder of myths and heroic legends setting forth beliefs about life and death, using Homer as an example.

Discuss how purposes and types of poetry are many and varied. Some are written for pleasure and some to teach important lessons. Define three types of poetry: lyric, dramatic, and narrative. Don't spend too much time on poetic form so as not to alienate the students. Have students write several poems. Have them select one poem and a setting where they will deliver the poem. Allow students to select from the church, cemetery, ballfield, cars, classrooms, parking lots, or wherever they feel a sense of connection. Videotape students reading their poems and then have them critique each others' poetry and delivery while watching the tape.

FOLLOW-UP ACTIVITY:
Have students select one poem to be set to music.
Write a new poem as a group.

RESOURCES:
Language of Life, Bill Moyers's video series on contemporary poets, 1996.
The Last Puritan, by George Santayana. Cambridge, MA: MIT Press, 1995.
Leaves of Grass, by Walt Whitman. New York: Bantam Classics, 1983.
The Name and Nature of Poetry, by A. E. Houseman. New York: New Amsterdam Books, 1989.
The Poetry of Robert Frost. New York: Henry Holt, and Co., 1979.
The Selected Poems of Emily Dickinson: The Modern Library Series. New York: Random House, Inc., 1998.

The Watershed Partnerships

The Watershed Partnerships program is a loose consortium of collaborations between colleges and universities and their local public schools. Participating teachers and students work together to conceive and implement curricula in environmental education. This program emphasizes convergence, between teachers and students of different age levels, between disciplines like science, art, history, and literature, and between work done in the classroom and in the field. Each Watershed Partnership is a gathering of energies and intelligences close to home, for the purpose of discovering, sharing, and celebrating the local environment.

The Watershed Partnerships grew out of the interest of two Middlebury College students, Tara Thomas and Virginia Lebermann, in carrying out an environmental education program in local schools. With support from The Orion Society and involvement of a talented Bristol, Vermont, teacher named Ann Straub, this project successfully pursued the integration of arts and sciences in a curriculum that also emphasized the local sense of place during the 1993-94 school year.

The following year saw an environmental studies seminar at Middlebury College, created around this model of partnering college students with local teachers. This seminar, which I dubbed "An Experiment in Environmental Education," met regularly to discuss readings by people like Rachel Carson, Edith Cobb, David Orr, and David Sobel (see appendix 1 for syllabus). The course also took pairs of Middlebury students on a weekly basis into almost every classroom at Bristol Elementary School, and culminated with a play and a community celebration focusing on the natural and human history of the town.

These partnerships in Bristol over a two-year period were exciting. The combination of reading, writing, drawing, measuring, classifying, experimenting, and mapping was heady. Every activity seemed enhanced by the others. College students loved seeing how their studies came together "on the ground," as well as being involved with local schoolchildren. They also gained a renewed appreciation for the creativity and the skill of the teachers in Bristol. Those teachers, for their part, were grateful for the enthusiasm and idealism—and the strong science backgrounds—of our students. And the schoolkids adored the college students, finding them glamorously ambiguous—full grown but neither parents nor regular teachers. They hurled themselves joyfully into the activities or outings that Middlebury students suggested.

These Bristol connections seemed valuable enough to merit expanding in two ways. In 1995-96 we placed pairs of Middlebury students in public schools all around Addison County, Vermont—not only in Bristol, but also in Salisbury, Lincoln, Monkton, and Starksboro. Mt. Abraham Union High School in Bristol was also involved in that year, as Middlebury Junior High School was in the following one. Simultaneously, we contacted a group of faculty members at other colleges and universities who had a special interest in environmental education. Those institutions, too, became the sites for what had become The Orion Society's Watershed Partnerships program. In 1995-96 and 1996-97, in addition to Middlebury College, they included Oberlin College, Rutgers University, Trenton State University, University of Vermont, Swarthmore College, Simon's Rock College, Teton Science School, and the University of New Mexico. At a conference in Vermont during the summer of 1996, representatives from the colleges and schools participating in the partnerships got together to compare notes. The partnerships, and their ambitious, field-based orientation, seemed to have worked wonderfully in many cases.

At the end of the 1996-97 academic year, the Orion staff and I agreed not to extend the Watershed Partnerships program. This was an expensive and time-consuming network to maintain, and in most cases, both among the point people at other college campuses and the teachers participating locally, those involved showed remarkable independence and reliability. So it seemed an appropriate time to consolidate what we had learned over this several-year sequence, write it up, disseminate it, and let people continue to forge partnerships in their own watersheds, attuned to whatever unique circumstances their communities provide.

John Elder

Getting to Know the Lake Champlain Bioregion

by Thomas R. Hudspeth

Professor of Environmental Studies
The University of Vermont
Burlington, VT

There was standing room only at Memorial Auditorium in Burlington, Vermont, on that crisp December evening. The governor of Vermont was there, as was the mayor of Burlington, 200 sixth-grade students from the Endeavor Team and seventh- and eighth-grade students from the Roots and Branches Team at Edmunds Middle School, their teachers and parents and siblings, countless interested community members, and twenty-six University of Vermont (UVM) students from my environmental education (EE) course, who had worked with the middle schoolers several hours per week throughout the fall semester. A reporter and photographer covered the event for the *Burlington Free Press*, and camera persons from two of the local television stations filmed the proud students standing beside their exhibits, explaining their research projects, and recounting their field trip experiences.

Their exhibits included: working models of a living machine and a tertiary wastewater treatment plant; displays of native plants and animals, the geology of Button Bay, aquatic nuisances in the Lake Champlain basin (zebra mussels, Eurasian milfoil, water chestnuts, purple loosestrife, etc.), non-point-source water pollution, an EPA Superfund site at the Burlington Barge Canal, wetlands in the basin, acid rain, shipwrecks in Lake Champlain, and Champ, Lake Champlain's very own mysterious bottom-dwelling creature. There were graphs comparing the quality of water they sampled from headwater streams on the summit of Mount Mansfield while on an overnight trip, from the LaPlatte River while on an all-day canoe trip, and from the Winooski River and Lake Champlain, as well as maps, artwork, poems, essays, photographs, and field

journals from their many field trips. They also had a
Hyperstudio computer presentation on the geology, plants, animals, and human history of Redstone Quarry. There were
viewings of a videotape of their time spent on Lake Champlain
aboard the UVM research vessel Melosira conducting tests of
turbidity, conductivity, temperature, and dissolved oxygen, and
another one of a mock New England town meeting role-play
simulation, where they considered the pros and cons of a proposed development adjacent to a significant wetland. Also on
display were plaster casts of animal tracks they had followed,
creation myths and stories they had written after listening to an
Abenaki storyteller, and photographs of salmon they had raised
from eggs in their classroom and released into rivers.

The event was the Lake Champlain Basin Community
Exposition, and it culminated the semester-long Watershed
Partnership between my EE students and six Burlington mid-
dle-school teachers and their students.

Many scientists have warned that the present decade may
be the last chance to reverse the downward environmental
trends and for humans to renegotiate their relationship with

the environment. Why, then, did these
middle school students and UVM students
focus their attention on their local bioregion—land of the Abenaki, the sugar
maple, the Green and Adirondack
Mountains, the Winooski River, Lake
Champlain, and the vibrant and progres-
sive city of Burlington—rather than studying such pressing environmental issues as
global warming, loss of biodiversity, tropi-
cal deforestation, desertification, ozone
depletion, overpopulation, and overcon-
sumption of resources? They were not
ignoring critical environmental concerns;
they were deliberately engaging in "place-
based EE" before attempting to deal with larger, more global
environmental problems.

Natural history, including physical properties such as geology, soils, weather patterns, climate; biological properties such as

native plants and animals; and cultural features, such as human settlement patterns, indigenous traditions, more recent human history, and ways people make their living from the land all contribute to the character of a place and help to define it. Place-based EE, also termed "locally based EE" or "locally focused EE," uses place as its unifying theme. Through what John Elder calls the "localized practice of attentiveness," students get to know the place where they live. Via direct, firsthand experience, they examine the natural features and cultural stories that make their place unique and special. They are exposed to the wonders and beauty of nearby nature, and are provided direct experience in the natural world that nourishes and encourages what Rachel Carson calls their "sense of wonder."

As students follow a local stream, track animals, make maps, and explore the climate, water systems, soil types, and native plants of their immediate environment, nature becomes less abstract and more concrete to them, and they are reminded that people are an integral part of nature and that we are all connected. Equally important is that students trace the human history and unique stories that their places have to tell. They make connections rooted in their own rich experiences and become grounded in the process.

By paying close attention to the character of their own homes, the students discover their sense of place, their connection with their surroundings, before turning their attention to the pressing environmental problems of the day. From studying events in their local watershed or bioregion, they gain a context for extending beyond to explore larger environments and environmental problems.

Heightened awareness of the local place from diligent study, exploration, and celebration leads to increased attachment, love, concern, devotion, care, respect, and sense of stewardship for it. The students develop what Aldo Leopold terms a "land ethic," an ethic of environmental stewardship. They feel a part of their local landscape and experience a sense of connectedness, of belonging to the community as citizens. This sense of community encourages the students to cultivate and sustain the unique qualities of their place, and provides an impetus for activism when the integrity of that environment becomes threatened.

During the fall semesters of 1995 and 1996, the twenty-six students in my environmental education courses at UVM and I had the good fortune to be selected for The Orion Society's Watershed Partnerships program. As part of the class, the students embarked on personal lifestyle changes aimed at lessening their negative impacts on the environment, made journal entries based on readings and homework assignments and in-class activities, conducted an analysis of an existing EE curriculum or program, visited an EE program or field trip or attended a conference or workshop, and carried out a term project.

The term project involved developing a place-based EE unit with at least six activities and field testing them with the partnering teachers and their students. The EE students generally worked in three- to five-person teams, coordinating the lesson and activities that they field tested at their partnering schools with each other. In 1995, all six teachers were part of teaching teams at Edmunds Middle School in Burlington. In 1996, there were two teachers at Edmunds, two at Hunt Middle School in Burlington, and two two-person teams offering environmental science classes at Burlington High School and South Burlington High School.

The partnering teachers appreciated the Watershed Partnership grants that allowed them to do things they might not otherwise have been able to do: go on field trips, purchase supplies and equipment, rent the auditorium for the expo, etc. They also appreciated the UVM students' help in the classroom and on field trips, and their enthusiasm and knowledge regarding the Lake Champlain basin, aquatic ecology, wetlands, living machines, and EE theory and practice (to which most of the participating teachers had little or no exposure). The teachers also thought it was important for their students to be exposed to positive role models such as the UVM students. The UVM students reported that they were very enthusiastically received by the partnering students whenever they went into the school.

All the UVM students kept journals for the EE class. From their entries, classroom discussions, and personal evaluations they were asked to write, I was able to learn the students' impressions. Virtually every student said the term project experience was a positive, worthwhile learning experience. They all claimed they were successful in accomplishing their objectives, and enjoyed the experience. They were grateful for the opportunity to "explore the world of teaching" and appreciated the exposure to role models in the partnering teachers. (In many cases, they indicated positive role models who were good teachers and who effectively handled difficult or rowdy children, or those with short attention spans. But in at least one case, they indicated a "control freak" role model who was far too punitive and behavior-modification oriented.)

> **As students explore their immediate environment, they are reminded that people are an integral part of nature and that we are all connected.**

They found it very rewarding to work with the partnering kids and experience what it is like to be in front of a class. Many mentioned that this was their first time actually teaching children, and admitted to having been nervous, apprehensive, unsure of themselves, even intimidated prior to leading their first activity, but felt that they gained increased confidence as a result. Many said the experience whetted their appetite; they looked forward to doing it again in the future, as it motivated them to pursue environmental education further. (Some followed this experience with semester-long internships at Shelburne Farms, Green Mountain Audubon Nature Center, Vermont Institute of Natural Science, and Keewaydin Environmental Education Center. A few students stayed on with their partnering teachers and classes during the spring semester to carry out a senior thesis or project.) However, a few said it reinforced their conviction not to be a public-school teacher.

Several students mentioned that they appreciated how the course mixed real-world practice with theory. They were truly able to confront the reality of a public-school classroom, with both its negative elements (e.g., behavior management issues; some unmotivated students; some surly, disrespectful students; scheduling blocks to deal with; numerous interruptions over the intercom system; outdated textbooks in some cases; little or no information on environmental topics in the classrooms or school library) as well as its positive elements (e.g., some highly motivated students who were already quite knowledgeable about environmental topics; some dedicated, enthusiastic teachers willing to schedule extra field trips; etc.). Quite a few students mentioned that their term project demonstrated how difficult it is to implement EE in the real world!

The UVM students tried to actively involve the Burlington kids instead of just lecturing at them; to lead the kids to answers instead of just providing them; to keep things interesting; to make the learning relevant to kids' lives—action-oriented, hands-on, discovery-based, interdisciplinary, cooperative, and fun. They recognized that teaching like this takes much time, energy, preparation, planning, and coordination; hence, the importance of pre-planning, of rehearsing, of dry runs, of having a structure. They acknowledged the importance of organization, of having sufficient resources, of having a fall-back/contingency plan, of being flexible, of taking advantage of the teachable moment, of appreciating different learning styles, of breaking down into small groups (or otherwise having good adult-to-children ratios), of getting down to the level of the children. Several emphasized the enormity of the task of being a good teacher, and commented on how draining it is. Virtually all the groups said that they wished they had started earlier and had more time to work with their partnering school class. They would have liked to have carried out all the activities in the unit they developed, from the beginning to the end, rather than just some of the lessons—this would have provided a greater sense of closure.

By its very nature, place-based EE is interdisciplinary, integrating writing and the arts with the natural sciences and social sciences. I feel that this Watershed Partnership between my EE students and the middle-school partners allowed for very successful instances of designing and implementing place-based examples of EE that enlivened the educational process. EE was infused into science, social studies, language arts, and mathematics classes, broadening the scope of otherwise narrow disciplines. Stories of the interrelationships between social, economic, political, historical, and ecological issues were woven together to reveal a tapestry of the interdependence of cultural and natural systems in a place. This inductive and comprehensive study of the environment unified students' experiences—rather than simply adding a new environmental studies unit—and provided a wholeness in learning that would not have been achieved otherwise.

Environmental Education Journal

GRADES: Undergraduates

OBJECTIVE:
Help environmental education students communicate or express their ideas more clearly and help them develop their skills of critical thinking and creativity.

MATERIALS:
Bound journals or notebooks

TIME NEEDED:
Have students keep their journals throughout the semester.

DESCRIPTION:
Explain the journal to your students. Journal writing is different from almost all other writing that you do in that its end is really the process of writing, rather than the written product itself. In your journal you engage in a form of writing known as "expressive writing." This is the form of writing closest to thought. It is the same as the voice that you use to talk to yourself all the time ("Uh oh! I can't believe I..."). In contrast, "transactive writing" is the form of writing that you use to communicate to others. While transactive writing must be clearly organized, and carefully worded, expressive writing can be raw—pure thought poured out onto the page.

The wonderful thing about journal keeping—as those of you who already keep journals know—is that it offers the opportunity to give full range to your ideas, exploring and clarifying your thinking in a way not possible without the written word; yet it frees you from the constraints of conforming your writing style to the standards necessary to communicate with others. In your journal, you become actively engaged with your ideas and experiences. Through the free-writing process you make connections, build relationships, focus, and stretch your thinking.

Have your students use the journal in several ways: to develop their thinking before class discussions, to process class events and activities personally, and to draw connections between read-ings and class discussions. Give students one or more assignments to write about in their journals at home each week. This will give them an opportunity to reflect on course ideas and experi-ences and to relate them to other parts of their lives. Explain that for each of these journal entries they should try to write continuously for a minimum of five minutes, or about a page (really continuously—without lifting their hands if possible!). Longer entries are even better, presenting an opportunity to develop thoughts, insights, ideas, and questions more fully.

Each journal entry should have a short identifying title and date. Students do not need to type journal entries. Collect the journals at various times during the semester and evaluate them, not in terms of writing style, but rather, on your students' com-mitment to the journaling process and on the depth with which they explore the ideas and experiences of the course.

In my experience, when students make frequent entries in their journals, and when they take those entries seriously, they will enjoy writing them. Their journals will make the class material more meaningful, more focused, and more fun. The more they write, the more they will be actively engaged in the subject. They will be writing what they choose to write and remember about your course.

EXAMPLES OF JOURNAL QUESTIONS:
1. What were some of your personal significant life experi-ences/formative influences with regard to the environment?

2. What experiences shaped the development of your own relationship with the natural world?

3. Carry out one of the activities in Michael Cohen's book *Connecting with Nature* (World Peace University Publishing, 1991), and reflect on it.

4. Questions based on Steve Van Matre, *Earth Education: A New Beginning* (Institute for Earth Education, 1990):
    1.) Do you feel it would be more effective to add EE to the curriculum as a separate course in, for example, grades

5, 8, and 11, or to infuse environmental education into all disciplines in the curriculum at all grade levels? Why?;
2.) Reflect upon your own exposure to environmental education, especially in school. Did it focus on the pieces, or on the process of how life functions?;
3.) How do you react to the "Principles of Deep Ecology"? Do you consider yourself to be a "shallow-environmentalist" or "deep ecologist" (or something else)? Why?;
4.) Who has influenced you by modeling positive environmental behaviors or leading by example? And what were some of the positive environmental behaviors they modeled?

5. What is your reaction to the following passage by Rachel Carson in *A Sense of Wonder*?

> If facts are the seeds that later produce knowledge and wisdom, then the emotions and the impressions of the senses are the fertile soil in which the seeds must grow.... Once the emotions have been aroused—a sense of the beautiful, the excitement of the new and the unknown, a feeling of sympathy, pity, admiration, or love—then we wish for knowledge about the object of our emotional response.

6. Have you found yourself "reconnecting with nature" in new or different ways as a result of leading students in "connecting with nature" activities?

7. Pick an activity from Joseph Cornell, *Sharing Nature with Children* (Dawn Publications, 1998) or *Sharing the Joy of Nature* (Dawn Publications, 1989); or Marina Herman, Joseph Passineau, Ann Schimpf, and Paul Treuer, *Teaching Kids to Love the Earth* (Pfieifer-Hamilton, 1991) that is appreciably different from a Cohen or Van Matre activity. Try it out with your partnering students and reflect on how effective you think it was at helping the students bond with nature.

8. Provide a personal evaluation of your term project, for which you designed placed-based EE activities and field tested them with your partnering teachers and their students as part of the Watershed Partnership. In your evaluation, address the following four items:

1.) Do you feel that your program succeeded in meeting its objectives? Why or why not?;

2.) How would you improve it if you were to run it again?;

3.) Were there surprises for you in working with a real group of learners and a supervising teacher, and, if so, what did you learn from them?;

4.) What "rules of thumb," techniques, strategies, and revelations about the field of EE and about yourself as an environmental educator will you carry away from this experience?

Finding Our Place on the Trail
by Alice Leeds

Lincoln Community School
Lincoln, VT
Grades 5-6

O ur small elementary school of just over 120 students sits along the New Haven River, looking up at the river's source on Mount Abraham. The students love their mountain town, its river and woodlands, its natural beauty, and the safe, close-knit community where houses spread out across the open landscape, and mountains, fields, and sky crisscross into each other to form a collage of color and texture.

In March of 1996, when the nature trail behind our school was still hidden beneath layers of white and spring was several daydreams away, we began the first of two environmental units supported by the Watershed Partnerships. Our unit focused on botany, and my fifth- and sixth-grade students labeled it PAPA Nature, an acronym for Plants, Animals, People, and Art. On our first afternoon with three Middlebury College environmental education students, the class joyfully trotted off into the woods. A cold rain was falling and the ground was slush covered. Shortly afterward, twenty wet students poured back into our classroom with red fingers and bright noses. On the first damp pages of their nature journals were drawings and poems that captured the energy and beauty of a March afternoon along the New Haven River. It was clear right away that many students found messages and comfort out there.

For several months, the students returned weekly to spots chosen as their own, recording observations, sketching the changing trees and plant life, and writing free-verse poems in their nature journals. Chris Gale, a sixth-grade boy, wrote:

> I see the river flowing.
> Gracefully. I sit in my spot

just looking at the calm water.
The river splits. One side goes one way,
the other side goes the other way,
but it is okay. The two sides meet
after the little island passes.
The river reminds me of the wind,
just going at its own pace, flowing.

Throughout the course of the unit, students were immersed in botanical projects. Our art teacher, Vera Ryersbach, guided students in paper making and drawing from nature. During math class we created tessellating shapes, defining and shading repeating forms that resembled trees, leaves, and flowers. We learned to use natural dyes made from onion skins and dandelions, experimenting with them on silk and cotton. (We discovered that silk absorbs color much more readily.) Student pairs designed and conducted grow lab experiments to determine the influence of various kinds and amounts of light, water, soil mediums, and space on plant growth. They carried out independent research projects on botany-related topics such as the paper industry and endangered plant species. The results of their many projects were displayed at an open house at the conclusion of our unit.

The highlight of the PAPA Nature unit was spending time on the trail and in the classroom with Middlebury College students Billy, Andy, and Sarah. We also enjoyed the support of parents and community members who helped us discover and identify emerging buds, patterns of erosion and succession, and signs of animal life, including a fresh bobcat track set in the soft bank of the river early one June morning. Gradually the weather improved enough so that we were able to gather and analyze data about trees and low growth. We examined broad ecological concepts, then got down to the task of writing about the ecosystems along the trail. The students' essays, along with their poems and drawings, culminated in a published nature journal.

When our class received another round of funding to participate in a second Watershed Partnership, the project benefited from the knowledge of our nine returning multi-age students.

The school year began with the bright heat of an Indian summer, but we all knew the fleeting nature of Vermont's autumn, so we scurried to make the most of our last few fine days.

This time, we carried out a cross-curricular unit on homes and architecture encompassing a wide array of projects. The students published a walking tour of ten historic houses in Lincoln Center. They carried out design-technology tasks to uncover basic structural concepts, then designed plans and built architectural models for their dream homes, incorporating the influence of the environment on their designs. After reading novels about homelessness, students created poetry and dance pieces to express their emotional responses. The work of sculptor Beverly Buchanan inspired students to create miniature dwellings from discarded and natural materials, and later students composed short vignettes based on the unseen residents of these dwellings.

For the environmental studies component, the class learned about animal homes, animal architecture, and the use of native materials in human dwellings. Two Middlebury College students, Wendy and Jess, worked with half the students two afternoons each week. Under their guidance, students made sound maps of the trail, searched for amphibians and land critters, and collected and observed water animals in the river. They simulated a bird's experience by taping their

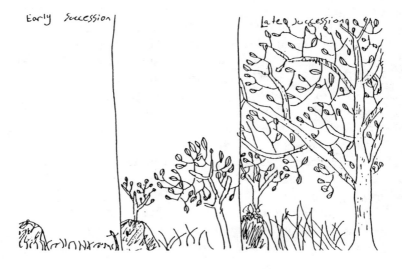

Early Succession

Late Succession

fingers together before attempting to build nests of twigs, pine needles, and leaves. They also moved a step beyond reality, creating detailed drawings of imaginary insects complete with descriptions of each one's habitat and food sources.

After becoming familiar with the habitats along our nature trail, each student chose one native animal to research and sketch. These drawings, along with their stories, became the basis for a winter advent calendar in which animals and stories were unfolded one by one from inside their nests, burrows, and dens in a student-painted mural.

Periodically, we held joint sessions with the full group. On one such occasion, the class viewed the video "Animal Architecture." In our subsequent discussion on principles of structure, students drew links between animal and human architecture. Later, students composed poems about home building written from the point of view of the animal. Hylda Rood, a sixth grader, wrote "Horse Fluff Bird's Nest" for this exercise, a poem based on the experience of grooming her horse:

> As I fly over the land I sing my beautiful song
> I see a young girl brushing and grooming a horse
> She takes a bit of fluff
> And holds it in her hand
> The wind grabs it from her hand, pulling it to the sky
> I swoop down and grab it
> Then fly to a nearby tree
> I drop the fluff on a branch
> Then fly down to the earth
> And pull 30 strands of long golden color grass
> Then I fly back to the tree
> I take the fluff and grass
> And start to build my cup-shaped nest
> When I am done I sit and lay my eggs
> Five beautiful bluish speckled eggs
> When they hatch my husband will find food
> And we both shall care for our young

This poem resulted in a collaborative poetry-dance piece presented at the open house for our homes and architecture unit.

Another joint session, and a highlight of the unit, was spent constructing debris huts along our nature trail. Students read through a collection of books on Native American homes built from native materials, then used these ideas to design a plan for their own shelters. Two crisp afternoons were spent constructing shelters from fallen twigs and branches and leaves. The first day was spent creating the "bones" of the structure, while the second session was used to cover them with some form of "skin." A number of students designed huts under or alongside the protection of low-hanging or thick trees, while others fashioned sturdy free-standing designs.

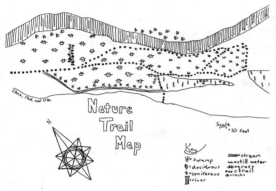

This activity struck a deep chord in all the students. Their resulting structures were playful and practical and incredibly unique. There were teepee and dome-shaped huts, longhouses and lean-tos, some just big enough for a tiny creature, while others could easily shelter two or three students. We returned to these huts throughout the changing seasons of our school year, repeatedly finding many of them fully intact. Crawling inside on a day in February, students noticed how the interiors provided insulation. We saw a mouse scurry out of a shelter one chilly afternoon.

After completing this second unit in the Watershed Partnership, I came upon new insights. I discovered how an environmental perspective can be used to address a topic that is not generally thought of as environmentally oriented. In the case of our homes unit, the environmental component added an exciting dimension to an already rich theme, and our students responded enthusiastically. Many of them thanked us repeatedly for experiences we offered them during this unit and referred back to them throughout the year.

People are a vital resource for addressing a classroom unit broadly and deeply. The rich experiences made available to our students could not have been planned, no less carried out, by a single individual. Our Middlebury interns' support in developing multifaceted environmental themes was a major benefit of our Watershed Partnership. Because of the impetus provided by the partnership, we reached out to discover that many community members were also glad to lend a hand.

On the afternoon before the last day of school, we took one last stroll together along the nature trail. Many of the debris huts built by students last fall were still standing, though the pine boughs placed across them had lost their needles. We walked past the structures and peered into them, looking for mice and gremlins and wondering if these huts would last into next fall. Like our year, some parts will sift away, while the places that have been built securely will remain, providing the recesses and ledges in which to place future experiences.

Spring Journal and Trail Guide

GRADE: Adaptable to any grade level

OBJECTIVE:
To document a portion of our nature study and to share our learning with other students and community members. Initially, we intended to create a trail guide, but the students decided to include creative reflections as well, after reading their classmates' wonderful journal entries.

MATERIALS:
Paper
Colored pencils and pens
Field guides
Copy shop for reproduction

TIME NEEDED:
Four weeks at the conclusion of the study of a nature trail.

DESCRIPTION:
Our guide contained three main sections. The first section discusses the ecosystems along our school's nature trail: river, marsh, and forest. The second section defines five ecological principles: ecosystems, succession, biodiversity, interdependence, and food webs. For the third section, each student submitted and illustrated a poem written during the course of the unit. The centerfold shows a student-created map of the trail.

During the last four weeks of our unit, students worked in pairs on one of the essays or the map. Over a time period of several weeks, essay groups recorded questions about their topics and attempted to answer them, using this information in their drafts. In revisions, they tried to convey their learning in a creative and compelling voice, to pull the reader into their experience of the trail. Meanwhile, the mapmakers created a scaled map, complete with symbols and a legend.

Our resources, in addition to the Middlebury College students, were field guides and community members. Over the course of the project, both in the classroom and along the trail, we were assisted by experts in the areas of geology, geography, botany, forestry, biology, entomology, and tracking. Before publication, several local naturalists read and commented on our drafts.

Each student was responsible for the layout of his or her pages. Throughout the unit, students worked on contour drawing under the guidance of our art teacher. Final sketches were rendered in pen. Students typed their poems and essays and made decisions about typefaces, formatting, and illustrations. We kept in mind that each final page would need to fit on the folded half of an 8.5 x 11-inch page.

For the cover, each student created a tiny color drawing using pen and colored pencils. These were arranged to fit the front and back pages of our class journal, leaving a small space for the title. We splurged and used a color copier for the cover. Two students composed an acknowledgments page and I wrote an introduction.

Our nature journal was distributed throughout the school and made available to community members at the town clerk's office. We hope that future Lincoln students will find the guide informative and satisfying reading, and that it may even inspire subsequent classes to spend some time on our school's nature trail.

Acquiring Felt Knowledge

by Nicole J. Greene

Middlebury College Graduate
Ophir, Colorado

A Megamid ("mid" for short) is a four-sided pyramid, a glo-rified tarp really, with a single aluminum pole holding it up—a tent without a floor. When raindrops thwap down on the nylon, it sounds like the noise made by clicking your tongue on the roof of your mouth. Lightning illuminates my little purple-and-white nylon home and I carefully count the seconds until the sky belches with a grumbling thunder. Twelve. Still safe. But keep track.

Having been out on the trail for sixteen days, I lie here within the confines of my mummy bag watching the mud splatter onto my bivy sack and think of my somewhat more glamorous college education. I'm certainly not attaining the goals that so many of my classmates were striving for: I'm not making much money, and Megamids don't offer much in terms of stability, or, for that matter, staying dry.

And yet, there is nowhere I would rather be. At times, I realize that what I do here high in the Colorado mountains as an Outward Bound instructor has very much to do with what I learned in my years at Middlebury College, in particular with a class that I took the first semester of my sophomore year. The class was called "An Experiment in Environmental Education," and was taught by John Elder. I had no idea what I was getting into when I signed up. I had no idea this class would change my life. We set out to read texts about environmental educa-tion and then to create our own activities for elementary school students. We were then paired with local teachers so that we could implement our programs in the classroom. Hands-on experiences in the classrooms of Bristol, Vermont, combined with rich discussions among my class members back in Middlebury, revealed to me the value of exposing children to the wonders of the natural world.

Only seven seconds between the lightning and thunder now. I drag my rain-soaked ensolite pad out of my Megamid and rouse my students from beneath their soggy tarps. Into the rain. We spread out into "lightning drill" formation. In their yellow Helly Hansen jackets, my students look like rubber duckies with the paint rubbed off. We count together as the lightning moves closer—until it can't be more than 100 yards away. I squat lower to the ground and hope.

When the wind begins to blow harder, I know that the storm is passing. Four seconds. Then nine. I help my dripping students secure their tarps, get a stove started for dinner, and we quickly debrief the exciting experience. I retreat to my mid.

There is never a lack of excitement in my work as an Outward Bound instructor. But that's not why I love it. That's not why I'm here squeezing the water out of my socks and picking the caked mud off of my legs. I am here because I have come to embrace the concepts of place-based experiential education through the harvest of my own experiences as a student, and as a teacher.

Peak experiences occur not just on the tops of mountains, but also in classrooms, in the field, and in other moments inherent in extraordinary education. It was my experiences in the classrooms of Bristol that led me to the revelatory realization that I am a teacher.

In Elder's class, we based our studies and student teaching on the premise that environmental education should focus on developing a sense of place through direct experience in the natural world—experience that is relational, reciprocal, and holistic. In and through this kind of interaction with their natural environments, young students acquire an appreciation for the sacredness of what Martin Buber calls the I-Thou relationship. Spontaneously, children seem to develop this kind of relationship with their own special places. The child who

spends hours in a vacant lot watching black beetles sway back and forth on long strands of yellow grass, and the one who always picks the same spot in the same tree in which to play during recess, both exhibit this kind of connection.

As a teacher, it is possible to facilitate the development of the I–Thou relationship. Encouraging students to find "special

spots" where they can go for a brief period of time each day to read, write, draw, or observe is an effective way to nurture a child's sense of wonder about place. Edith Cobb, author of *The Ecology of Imagination in Childhood*, believes that a child's experience with place often fosters "an awareness of one's own unique separateness and identity, and also a continuity, a renewal of relationship with nature," and ultimately, with all things.

From my experiences teaching, I know this to be true. I have seen students who never seemed interested in a single classroom subject come alive with curiosity and enthusiasm while sitting and watching birds flying overhead, playing with slimy aquatic insects, or examining the fragility of tree bark. Through the Watershed Partnerships in Bristol, we made time each day for our students to visit their special spots. These various nooks and crannies of the playground became intimately a part of each child's life, and by the end of the semester, the students actually chose to have extra time in their spots rather than participating in playground games.

One day in particular stands out in my mind. My fourth graders and I were walking back to the school building after doing a poetry activity at our special spots. A young girl named Sarah came up to me and nestled her small hand into the curve of my own. "There is so much to look at in nature," she said. "When I go past in a car, it never seems like there's much to see, but when you really look, there's tons." I watched as she turned her face up to the sky. "But it's hard to put the way it makes me feel into words."

"What did you write about?" I asked, gesturing toward the

piece of crinkled notebook paper in her other hand.

"It's a poem about the trees."

"How do the trees make you feel?" I asked, bending down so I could look her in the eyes.

"Alive, the trees make me feel alive," she said with a smile. The glimmer in Sarah's eyes lit up that gray Vermont day. This is why I am here, I thought to myself as I squeezed her hand.

To this day, the look in Sarah's eyes lingers in my mind as an inspiration. In order to facilitate these kinds of experiences, we should nourish our children not merely with facts and figures but with opportunities to acquire "felt knowledge." Through direct interaction and healthy relationships with people and nature, children learn the value of respect, compassion, and strong relationships. When nurtured, a child's desire to learn matures into an adult's sense of place, sense of community, and sense of self.

Through the process of examining environmental education curricula in preparation for the classes I would teach in Bristol, I realized that too often elementary schools create programs to teach students about environmental degradation and global issues such as ozone depletion, global warming, and rainforest destruction. The goal is to produce educated environmental citizens who can contribute to society through their voting and purchasing power. But the effect is proving to be just the opposite, as David Sobel suggests in *Beyond Ecophobia*. By inundating young students with information about environmental destruction, we may in fact "be engendering a subtle form of dissociation," somewhat similar to the kind of detachment from pain that children experience when they watch gratuitous violence on TV, or in more extreme instances, are victims of physical or sexual abuse. If we only teach children about the terrible ways humans have treated the earth, we may in effect only foster fear—fear of being anywhere near nature.

In my work with the students in Bristol, I came to realize that place-based study can be the connective tissue of a truly interdisciplinary curriculum. We were not teaching environmental education but instead were educating the young students about their homes. We examined local plants, did animal tracking projects, mapped our backyards, traced our water from

precipitation to tap, and looked at local sources of food.
Through writing, painting, dancing, singing, and creating music
we wove our studies together with an artistic thread. In this
rich confluence of disciplines and ideas, the students of Bristol
developed an understanding of and appreciation for their place.

Wholeness in learning is vital. In his essay "The Land
Ethic," Aldo Leopold writes that it is impossible "that an
ethical relation to the land can exist without love, respect and admiration for the land, and a high regard for its value." Or, as Paul Knoop put it,

> **Through direct interaction and healthy relationships with people and nature, children learn the value of respect, compassion, and strong relationships.**

"nothing will suffice, short of teaching people to love."
Direct experience in nature provides the context for this
kind of learning—in which it is affection that binds the student to his or her subject matter.

This is where the most fundamental change in education
must take place. Through my experiences in the classrooms of
Bristol, Vermont, I realized that effective education is not
defined by just being able to answer the questions at the end
of the chapter. Instead, education should be relevant, experi-
ence-based, hands on, and participatory. I believe fundamental-
ly in the power of this kind of education to enkindle a sense
of wonder, a desire to learn, and a respect for place. This belief
has inspired me to make it my life. In my work for the
Colorado Outward Bound School, and in my current position
as the Watershed Education Coordinator for the Telluride
Institute in southwestern Colorado, I facilitate these kinds of
experiences—where nature is the true teacher.

Back in the Colorado Rockies, the pot that I placed at the
base of my Megamid to catch the raindrops cascading off the
nylon is almost full. I marvel at my ingenuity as I fill yet
another water bottle with fresh rain water. As I reach to return
my pot for another fill, I notice two rain-soaked leather hiking
boots outside my mid.

"Nicole, it's Katherine. I'm really wet, but do you think I

could come in?" ask the feet.

"Of course," I unzip the long zipper and hold the wet nylon aside for the dripping ducky to waddle her way into my home.

"What's up?" I ask as I pull her yellow hood back far enough so that I can see her pooling eyes.

"You know, for the last sixteen days that we've been out here, I've watched you and wondered—wondered why you are here, why you would choose this for your lifestyle," Katherine said intently, as if there were nothing I could say or do to disrupt her train of thought. The same girl who refused to sit on the ground the first three days of the course didn't seem to notice the drops of water that were falling on her forehead from a leak in the seam of my mid, or that when she put her hand down on the ground it sunk two inches into the dark mud.

"And after tonight's storm, do you think it's even more crazy?" I asked, expecting giggling agreement.

"No, that's just the thing. That's how I should feel, that's how I thought I would feel, but I don't." She paused to wipe her eyebrows with her muddy hand, smearing dirt across her wet forehead.

"For the first time, I think I understand," and she looked up at me as if to take in my presence for the first time.

Finding Home: A Mapping Activity

> To explore memory, you have to be a good archae-
> ologist, knowing where and how to dig. The pur-
> pose of revisiting the special places of childhood is
> to gain awareness of the connections we make
> with the earth, awakening and holding these mem-
> ories in our consciousness of the present.
> —Mitchell Thomashow
> *Ecological Identity*

GRADES: Adaptable to any grade level

OBJECTIVE:
This activity engages students in mapping their homes and
including any places of significance. It offers students the
chance to identify with the special places that have been an
important part of their childhood experience.

MATERIALS:
Pens, pencils, markers, crayons, etc.
One large piece of paper for each student
A blank wall on which to display finished maps (Encourage
your students to make their maps beautiful!)

TIME NEEDED:
15 minutes to introduce the activity
30 minutes to an hour to map (can be given as a homework
assignment)
30 minutes to an hour to share maps (depends on the number
of students in the class)
30 minutes to an hour to discuss maps (you may want to take
more time with older students)

DESCRIPTION:
Everyone has a different perception of the place where they
live and how they choose to interact with their natural environments and biological communities. In the words of the

photographer Tony King, "Why we love a place has more to do with us than with the place. It is our experience that binds us to geography." In the same way, we each come to view our places with a different set of values, each one's perception having a unique significance to the whole. Mapping helps to bring awareness to these differences and enables students to express an individual relationship with the place where they live.

This is the kind of activity that students learn from most when it is appropriately framed to give purpose to the task. Often a good way to introduce the project is for the teacher to present his or her own map. Teachers should encourage their students to include any places or geographic features, near or far, that are of particular relevance to their personal experience.

Note that too much structure can inhibit creativity, but too little gets poor results. With this activity especially, it is important to find the right balance. The final products are often very telling. Some students include areas on their maps that are far away, whereas others can fill an entire page with an intricate map of their backyard.

Students enjoy sharing their maps and revealing their special places to the rest of the group, which is great fuel for a group discussion on place. Teachers can facilitate this kind of conversation by asking questions like: Why is a specific place more important than others? How has that place contributed to who you are? Do your special places tend to be natural or human made? What is it that makes your special places special? These kinds of questions lead students to think about the importance of special places in their lives, and notice how they have contributed to their individuality.

FOLLOW-UP ACTIVITIES:
Writing assignments about special childhood places.
Have students draw their special places.
Have students write how they would feel if their special places were in some way threatened (this can promote an interesting discussion about environmental and development issues).

SUPPLEMENTARY STUDENT READING:
The Giving Tree, by Shel Silverstein. New York: HarperCollins, 1986.
All the Places To Love, by Patricia MacLachlan. New York: HarperCollins, 1994.

SUGGESTED REFERENCES:
Children's Special Places: Exploring the Role of Forts, Dens and Bush Houses in Middle Childhood, by David Sobel. Tucson, AZ: Zephyr Press, 1992.
Ecological Identity: Becoming a Reflective Environmentalist, by Mitchell Thomashow. Cambridge, MA: MIT Press, 1995.
The Ecology of Imagination in Childhood, by Edith Cobb. Dallas, TX: Spring Publications, 1993.
The Geography of Childhood: Why Children Need Special Places, by Gary Paul Nabhan and Stephen Trimble. Boston: Beacon Press, 1994.

Appendix 1: Watershed Partnerships Syllabus

ES 302
Spring Term, 1996
Middlebury College
John Elder

Environmental Education: A Bioregional Approach

This course combines a seminar on environmental education with internships in local schools. Working in cooperation with the teachers to design and implement place-based curricula will thus complement our reading and writing for the class. ES 302 is part of a consortium called the Watershed Partnerships, sponsored by The Orion Society and funded by the Geraldine R. Dodge Foundation.

Bioregional thinkers like Gary Snyder have developed a land-based model of culture, in which the insights of geology, biology, weather, indigenous traditions, and more recent historical experience all contribute to an inclusive sense of place. Environmental education that begins with attentiveness to our community's specific environment and history, that pursues an interdisciplinary curriculum, and that integrates study out of doors can provide an encouraging alternative to more problem-based or controversial approaches. In our partnerships this semester, we will doubtless take widely differing approaches, but the practice of local attentiveness will be our common ground.

Students in ES 302 will have the following formal responsibilities: preparation for and participation in all sessions of the seminar; weekly written responses to the reading and to their experiences in the schools; two more formal essays; preparation for and contribution to four to five hours in the schools each week, as scheduled with the teachers; and an oral presentation with your partners, based on your internships.

The informal writings will take the form of two one-to-two page entries each week—one responding to the reading for a given session and the other reporting about and evaluating recent experiences at the schools. The first formal essay will relate one of the books or essays discussed in class to your own experiences and insights from the internship. It should be seven to ten pages in length. The second essay should be of the same length. In it, you should reflect upon some issue in environmental education that has assumed special importance to you, and make reference to any readings or experiences that help you bring the topic into sharp focus.

Readings

"E Is for Ecosystem," by David Quammen, from *Outside* Magazine (August 1994)

"Enviro Education," by Patricia Poore, from *Garbage* Magazine (April/May 1993)

"An Explosion of Green," by Bill McKibben, from *The Atlantic Monthly* (April 1995)

"The Otter Creek Watershed" from *Otter Creek Journal* (Spring 1994)

"A Wilderness of Scars," by John Elder, from *Wild Earth* (Summer 1995)

Beyond Ecophobia, by David Sobel (The Orion Society, 1996)

Children's Special Places, by David Sobel (Zephyr Press, 1992)

Earth in Mind, by David Orr (Island Press, 1994)

Ecological Identity, by Mitchell Thomashow (MIT Press, 1995)

Ecological Literacy, by David Orr (SUNY Press, 1992)

The Ecology of Imagination in Childhood, by Edith Cobb (Spring Publications, 1993)

Orion Magazine, "The Place Where You Live," Spring 1995.

The Geography of Childhood, by Gary Paul Nabhan and Stephen Trimble (Beacon Press, 1994)

The Practice of the Wild, by Gary Snyder (North Point Press, 1991)

A Sense of Wonder, by Rachel Carson (Harper & Row, 1956)

Appendix 2: Resources

REFERENCES:

The Art of Field Sketching, by Clare Walker Leslie. Dubuque, IA: Kendall/Hunt, 1995.

Being in the World: An Environmental Reader for Writers, edited by Scott Slovic. New York: Prentice Hall, 1993.

Beyond Ecophobia, by David Sobel. Great Barrington, MA: The Orion Society, 1996.

Drawing on the Right Side of the Brain, by Betty Edwards. Los Angeles: Jeremy P. Tarcher, Inc., 1989.

Earth in Mind, by David Orr. Washington, DC: Island Press, 1994.

Ecological Identity, by Mitchell Thomashow. Cambridge, MA: MIT Press, 1995.

Ecological Literacy, by David Orr. Albany, NY: SUNY Press, 1992.

The Ecology of Imagination in Childhood, by Edith Cobb. Dallas, TX: Spring Publications, 1993.

Family of Earth and Sky, edited by John Elder and Hertha Wong. Boston: Beacon Press, 1996.

Finding Home, edited by Peter Sauer. Boston: Beacon Press, 1992.

The Geography of Childhood, by Gary Paul Nabhan and Stephen Trimble. Boston: Beacon Press, 1994.

Hands-On Nature: Information and Activities for Exploring the Environment with Children, by Jenepher Linglebach. Woodstock, VT: Vermont Institute of Natural Science, 1986.

Keepers of the Animals, by Joseph Bruchac and Michael Caduto. Golden, CO: Fulcrum Publishing, 1991.

Keepers of the Earth, by Joseph Bruchac and Michael Caduto. Golden, CO: Fulcrum Publishing, 1989.

Keepers of Life, by Joseph Bruchac and Michael Caduto. Golden, CO: Fulcrum Publishing, 1994.

A Life in Hand, by Hannah Hinchman. Salt Lake City, UT: Peregrine Smith Books, 1991.

Reading the Forested Landscape, by Tom Wessels. Woodstock, VT: The Countryman Press, 1997.

The Practice of the Wild, by Gary Snyder. San Francisco: North Point, 1991.

A Sand County Almanac, by Aldo Leopold. New York: Ballantine Books, 1991.

A Sense of Wonder, by Rachel Carson. New York: Harper & Row, 1956.

Sharing Nature with Children, by Joseph Cornell. Nevada City, CA: Dawn Publications, 1998.

CURRICULUM PROJECTS:

Black River Watershed Education Partnership Project
Oberlin College in partnership with Seventh Generation
25 Lake Avenue
Elyria, OH 44035

Journeys: A Sense of Place Curriculum
Teton Science School
P.O. Box 68
Kelly, WY 83011

The Private Eye, by Kerry Ruef
The Private Eye Project
7710 31st Ave. NW
Seattle, WA 98117

Project Aquatic
Western Regional Environmental Education Council, Inc.
5430 Grosvenor Lane
Bethesda, MD 20814

Project Learning Tree
American Forest Foundation
1250 Connecticut Avenue, NW, Ste. 320
Washington, DC 20036

Project Wild
Western Regional Environmental Education Council, Inc.
5430 Grosvenor Lane
Bethesda, MD 20814

The Rio Grande River Curriculum
Project Crossroads
Rt. 7, Box 124-TR
Santa Fe, NM 87505

River of Words
National Poetry and Art Contest and Curriculum
International Rivers Network
1847 Berkeley Way
Berkeley, CA 94703

San Miguel Watershed Education Project
The Telluride Institute
P.O. Box 1770
Telluride, CO 81435

The Selbourne Project
Roger Tory Peterson Institute

311 Curtis Street
Jamestown, NY 14701

Sharing the Skagit
North Cascades Institute
2105 Highway 20
Sedro-Woolley, WA 98284

The Ways of the Watersheds, by Kathleen Haskin
Frost Valley YMCA
2000 Frost Valley Road
Claryville, NY 12725

The ORION Society

THE ORION SOCIETY is an environmental education organization, an award-winning publisher, and a communications and support network for grassroots environmental and community organizations across North America. It is a nonprofit membership organization with 7,000 members, individual and organizational, representing all fifty states and fifteen foreign countries.

The Orion Society's work covers a broad educational spectrum, including summer teaching institutes, reading tours, conferences, model classroom programs that have introduced hundreds of teachers in over thirty states to principles of "place-based" education, and award-winning publications that seek to expand our understanding of our relationship with the natural world.

PROGRAMS

Orion Institutes, designed to teach teachers more effective ways of bringing nature study into the classroom and classroom study into nature.

Stories in the Land Teaching Fellowships, awarded to outstanding teachers for the design of interdisciplinary, place-based curricula.

The Forgotten Language Tour, which brings leading nature writers and poets to communities around the country for workshops and public readings.

Conferences, such as the historic Watershed Conference held in 1996 at the Library of Congress.

The Orion Grassroots Initiative, which provides fundraising, networking, and other communications and support services to member organizations around the country.

The John Hay Award, an annual award for significant

achievement in three areas: environmental writing, education, and conservation.

The Olivia Ladd Gilliam Award, an annual award for work in the fine arts that has made a significant contribution toward the deepening of our individual and cultural bonds to the natural community of life.

ONLINE RESOURCES

The Orion Society's Award-Winning Website (www.orion-society.org) hosts a variety of resources for teachers and grassroots activists: calendars of events, listings of other organizations working toward similar goals, and access to the Nature Literacy Library list of recommended environmental writing.

The Commons is an online discussion group dedicated to exploring the role of people in nature from a wide variety of perspectives.

EnviroArts: Orion Online (www.envirolink.org/enviroarts), is a website that hosts a collection of poetry, essays, stories, and photographic portfolios, gleaned largely from the pages of our two magazines, *Orion* and *Orion Afield*.

PUBLICATIONS

Orion, an award-winning quarterly magazine, features essays, fiction, poetry, photographs, and artwork that celebrate the relationship between people and the natural world. Each issue includes a thematic special section as well as a host of regular departments from reviews and profiles to portfolios of artwork.

Orion Afield, a new quarterly publication devoted to grassroots environmental initiatives in conservation, restoration, and education, balances the literary and artistic approach of *Orion* with environmental success stories, how-to information, and other resources for activists.

Finding Home offers a collection of the best essays from the first ten years of *Orion* Magazine. America's foremost nature writers explore the cutting edge of ecological thought, tracing the evolution of biological and spiritual bonds between culture and nature.
Price: $16.

Bringing the World Alive is an annotated bibliography of nature stories for children that reflect and celebrate the realm of the child and the natural world, while presenting ecological information in ways children can relate to and appreciate.
Price: $6.

Beyond Ecophobia by David Sobel is the first volume of the Nature Literacy Series. It speaks to teachers, parents, and others interested in helping children understand and care for nature, and includes descriptions of developmentally appropriate environmental education activities and a list of related children's books.
Price: $6.

Join Us!

All of our work requires the support of our membership. Please join us and for only $25 you will receive a year's subscription to *Orion* and *Orion Afield*.

For more information about Orion Society programs, write:

> The Orion Society
> 195 Main Street
> Great Barrington, MA 01230
> orion@orionsociety.org

Membership and Book Order Form

Yes! I would like to support the programs and publications of The Orion Society and receive one year (four issues each) of *Orion* and *Orion Afield*. Basic membership is $25. We appreciate any additional support that you might provide.

- ❏ $25 (member)
- ❏ $50 (supporter)
- ❏ $100 (donor)

- ❏ $500 (benefactor)
- ❏ $1000 (major benefactor)
- ❏ Other _____

Members giving $50 or more also receive (choose one):

- ❏ *Finding Home*
- ❏ Orion Society 100% Cotton T-shirt (*L and XL only*)

Members giving $100 or more may also provide a free gift membership to a friend (please enclose name and address).

Finding Home	_____ copies @ $16.00 each	_____
Bringing the World Alive	_____ copies @ $6.00 each	_____
Beyond Ecophobia	_____ copies @ $6.00 each	_____
Stories in the Land	_____ copies @ $8.00 each	_____
	Subtotal	_____
	Less 10% for Orion Society Members	_____
	Shipping (*$2 for first item, $1 each additional*)	_____
	Membership (*amount of donation box checked*)	_____
	For each membership outside U.S., please add $10 (Canada and Mexico) or $20 (foreign air mail)	_____
	Total (U.S. dollars only)	_____

Your address and payment information:

_____
Name

_____
Address

_____
City/State/Zip
Credit Card Number _____ Exp. Date _____

Send to: The Orion Society, 195 Main Street, Great Barrington, MA 01230